ULTIMATE
BOOK OF
TRIVIA

· ULTIMATE ·

BOOK OF

TRIVIA

The Essential Collection

OF OVER 1,000 CURIOUS FACTS TO IMPRESS
YOUR FRIENDS AND EXPAND YOUR MIND

BY SCOTT McNEELY

ILLUSTRATIONS BY ARTHUR MOUNT

CHRONICLE BOOKS

SAN FRANCISCO

Library of Congress Cataloging-in-Publication Data

McNeely, Scott.
   Ultimate book of trivia : the essential collection of over 1,000 curious facts to impress your friends and expand your mind / by Scott McNeely.
      pages cm
   ISBN 978-1-4521-3661-5 (hardback : alkaline paper)
   1. Curiosities and wonders. 2. Handbooks, vade-mecums, etc. I. Title.
   AG243.M3185 2015
   031.02—dc23

2014047355

Manufactured in China

Book design by Amanda Sim and Neil Egan
Additional Typesetting by Frank Brayton
Illustrations by Arthur Mount

10 9 8 7 6 5 4 3 2 1

Chronicle Books LLC
680 Second Street
San Francisco, CA 94107
www.chroniclebooks.com

Chronicle books and gifts are available at special quantity discounts to corporations, professional associations, literacy programs, and other organizations. For details and discount information, please contact our premiums department at corporatesales@chroniclebooks.com or at 1-800-759-0190.

For putting up with my frequent "Hey you guys, did you know . . . ?" moments of discovery while writing the *Ultimate Book of Trivia*, I dedicate this work to my very patient family: Aimee, Hollis, and Emmett.

CONTENTS

CONTENTS

Foreword

Why did I write the *Ultimate Book of Trivia*?

A long time ago, my friend Tom and I were sitting around the kitchen table talking about nothing in particular. The conversation turned, and Tom regaled me with the unexpected story behind the phrase "son of a gun," which was originally an unkind epithet meaning a child of uncertain paternity born aboard a ship.

In that moment at the kitchen table an idea was born: Wouldn't it be fun to write an entire book about weird and random facts that most people have never heard of? Wouldn't it be fun to shine a spotlight on the oddball curiosities and uncharted miscellany of the world in which we live?

Trivia books already exist, of course, but they're generally tedious and often trivial in the worst sense, with a stifling emphasis on bland facts and raw statistics. Do you care that Thomas Jefferson was the very first secretary of state? Do you care that Death Valley is the eighth-lowest place on Earth? Do you care that kangaroos are marsupials?

To be interesting, facts and stats must tell a story. Interesting facts should give insight into something you didn't know you wanted to know—or something you wish you had never known! What's the longest time somebody has kept his eyes open without blinking? Which U.S. president allowed pet alligators in the White House? What country briefly—and disastrously—switched to a Base 9 currency in the 1980s? How many rodent hairs and insect fragments do the U.S. Food and Drug Administration allow in a bar of chocolate?

Hey! *Now* you've got my attention.

I won't pretend that you'll be any smarter after reading the *Ultimate Book of Trivia*. But I can promise you one thing—you will be a lot more interesting to talk to.

Is everything in the *Ultimate Book of Trivia* true?

Yes, to the best of my knowledge. I have verified every fact using primary sources where possible, including websites run by the U.S. government, the United Nations, NASA, and the Centers for Disease Control and Prevention. In other cases I have relied on secondary sources, including mainstream news outlets such as the BBC, CNN, *Time, Newsweek,* and the *New York Times*; authoritative websites run by the likes of the Smithsonian, *National Geographic, Rolling Stone, Scientific American, Billboard,* and the Internet Movie Database (IMDB); plus respected online dictionary and encyclopedia sites such as Wikipedia and the Oxford dictionaries.

No doubt I got a few facts wrong. I apologize in advance for the inevitable inaccuracies.

—Scott McNeely

A Brief History of Trivia

Are you one of those people who think trivia is synonymous with useless facts? It's embarrassing to say, but you're partly right. Trivia has never been *useful*.

The word "trivia" itself is a modern invention. It didn't exist until the early twentieth century. And since the very beginning, trivia has connoted information of little importance. Consistently and stubbornly, trivia has been preoccupied by trifles and unimportant matters.

What changed?

In the 1950s quiz shows such as *Twenty One* and *The $64,000 Question* took television by storm. The concept was simple: award large cash prizes to "regular" people in dramatic question-and-answer formats. For a time quiz shows eclipsed *I Love Lucy* and *The Ed Sullivan Show* in popularity—until the infamous "quiz show scandals" of 1956, when it was revealed that contestants on some of the most popular programs were given answers in advance.

The premiere of *Jeopardy!* in 1964 reinvigorated knowledge-based shows. So, too, did the publication in 1966 of the book *Trivia*, which became a *New York Times* bestseller. The trivia craze was reborn.

 **Did you know?**

The word "trivia" is derived from the Latin *trivium*. It means "three ways" or "meeting of three ways," and it was the name given to the introductory curriculum—grammar, rhetoric, and logic—at medieval universities. The *trivium* was the basis of medieval higher education and a precursor to studying the more advanced *quadrivium*: arithmetic, geometry, astronomy, and music.

In the brief history of trivia, nothing compares to the night in 1979 when two Canadian journalists, Scott Abbott and Chris Haney, abandoned a frustrating game of Scrabble (the board was missing a handful of letters) and invented what would become one of the most successful board games in history: Trivial Pursuit.

The game debuted in Canada in 1982 and was an instant success. The first American edition was released in 1983 and sold more than 20 million copies within a year (to put that number into perspective, Michael Jackson's hit album *Thriller* sold 25 million copies in 1983).

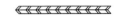

Scott Abbott purchased a racehorse and a Canadian hockey team with the money he earned from co-inventing the game Trivial Pursuit.

Trivial Pursuit single-handedly revived the fading board-game business. It also paved the way for like-minded games such as Pictionary, Scattergories, and Cranium. All of these games owe a heavy debt to Trivial Pursuit for convincing game makers—and consumers—that knowledge-based games can be fun and entertaining.

One downside to Trivial Pursuit's success? It's led some people to think trivia is little more than a mastery of obscure dates and anodyne facts.

Yet trivia is more than showing off a superior knowledge of useless things. Trivia tugs at your emotions, makes you writhe in ecstasy (yes! you know the correct answer) or despair (ack! it's right there on the tip of your tongue), and opens a window onto shared cultural and childhood experiences.

At its best trivia is both intensely rewarding and culturally cathartic. Sure it's not often useful—just don't call it boring!

⫸⫸⫸⫸ Three Tips for a Successful Pub Quiz ⫷⫷⫷⫷

Craving a rush of trivia-fueled adrenaline? You don't need to stay home playing Trivial Pursuit. More likely than not there is a pub quiz happening tonight at a nearby bar or pub. These events are wonderfully social and provide an opportunity to satisfy your quest for trivial knowledge without seeming too nerdy.

Here are three of the most important things to know about trivia nights.

1 You need a team. Pub quizzes are not like solitaire and should not be played with me, myself, and I. Gather some friends or, better yet, sit down at any table and introduce yourself. Trivia enthusiasts are usually open-minded and welcoming.

2 You need a team name. Some teams play for the glory of their homeland ("Aussie Aussie Aussie") or for the glory of alcohol ("Know It Ales"). Names such as "I Can't Read That" and "My Friends in the Corner" are guaranteed to amuse everybody except the quizmaster, who must recite your team name and scores out loud.

3 You need a sense of fairness. It's fair to bring your smart friends. It's not fair to use a phone to search the Internet for answers or look at other teams' answers.

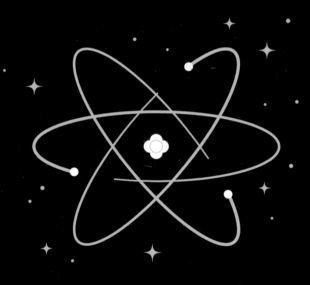

SPACE

SCIENCE

Space & Science

TRUE OR FALSE?

The first earthling in space was named Little Curly.

TRUE.

Kudryavka (Little Curly) was a terrier sent aboard the *Sputnik 2* spacecraft in 1957. Her food came in a gel, she pooped in a bag, and she had enough room to lie down. No wonder her name was later changed to Laika (Barker).

TRUE OR FALSE?

No living organism can survive in the vacuum of space.

FALSE.

In an experiment aboard the Soyuz spacecraft, lichen were exposed to space for fifteen days and survived.

TRUE OR FALSE?

NASA uses the same rocket technology used by TIE fighters in the *Star Wars* saga.

TRUE.

TIE stands for "twin ion engine"; ion engines are what propel NASA's *Deep Space 1* probe, launched in 1999.

TRUE OR FALSE?

Double-sun star systems like that found on Luke Skywalker's home planet of Tatooine really exist.

TRUE.

Scientists have found dozens of so-called "binary star systems" in the Milky Way galaxy alone.

TRUE OR FALSE?

The *Millenium Falcon's* jump to light speed in the *Star Wars* films is lethal. Nobody—including Han Solo and Chewbacca—could survive it given the laws of physics and gravity.

TRUE.

Accelerating from any terrestrial speed to anywhere near the speed of light causes inertia to fatally compress your body against your seat. To safely jump to light speed would require accelerating over a period of months.

➤ **WHICH OF THE FOLLOWING *STAR WARS* TECHNOLOGIES DOES NOT CURRENTLY EXIST?**

A Jedi hover bikes

B Star cruiser laser canons

C Floating alien probes

D Light sabers

ANSWER

D. Lasers are silent, unlike the light sabers in *Star Wars*. Nobody has yet figured out how to make lasers crash into each other with a *kschhhhhhh* sound.

TRUE OR FALSE? The *Star Wars* planet Alderaan, the destroyed home planet of Princess Leia, has a twenty-four-hour day and 365-day year, just like Earth.

TRUE.

TRUE OR FALSE? Venus's day is longer than its year.

TRUE.

It takes longer for Venus to rotate on its own axis than it does to complete one orbit around the sun.

TRUE OR FALSE? On Venus, the sun rises in the east and sets in the west.

TRUE.

TRUE OR FALSE? There is water on Mars.

TRUE.

In the form of ice.

TRUE OR FALSE? A lightning bolt on Earth is hotter than the surface of the sun.

TRUE.

Lightning bolts are actually five times hotter than the surface of the sun.

TRUE OR FALSE? A bolt of lightning on Earth packs enough energy to run a toaster for eighty-four thousand minutes, or roughly the amount of time it takes to toast 100,000 pieces of bread.

TRUE.

TRUE OR FALSE? Scientists are developing a high-energy laser beam that will trigger rain or lightning in a cloud zapped by the beam.

TRUE.

Water condensation and lightning are triggered by charged particles in a cloud, which can be stimulated by a laser.

TRUE OR FALSE? You wouldn't notice a difference if the sun were made of popcorn. Or bananas.

TRUE.

Believe it or not, it matters little whether the sun is made of hydrogen gas, popcorn, bananas, or old shoes. The sun's mass is so large, and its internal pressure so intense, that it squeezes its mass into a gaseous plasma that generates heat and energy. So for a short period of time, it wouldn't matter what the sun was made of. As long as it had the same mass, it would generate the same amount of heat and energy. The only caveat here: a popcorn or banana sun would not generate a self-sustaining fusion reaction like our hydrogen-fueled sun, and thus it would cool down quickly and burn out.

 **Did you know?**

Weight is relative, because weight simply measures the downward force of your body's mass. Which means you'd be really, really fat if you lived on the sun: A 150-pound earthling weighs in at 4,200 pounds on the sun's surface.

TRUE OR FALSE? More than one thousand Earths would fit inside Jupiter.

TRUE.

Jupiter is really big.

TRUE OR FALSE? All the other planets in the solar system would fit inside Jupiter—twice.

TRUE.

And remember: Jupiter is really big.

TRUE OR FALSE? There is no gravity in deep space.

FALSE.

While gravity weakens at a distance, there is gravity everywhere in the universe.

TRUE OR FALSE? "Spaghettification" is the name for the theoretical process by which objects are pulled apart by gravity as they fall into black holes.

TRUE.

TRUE OR FALSE? Teleportation is possible using today's technology.

TRUE.

It's already happened. Scientists have transported individual atoms using quantum entanglement. Just don't book your next trip to Paris on a teleporter. It's far more complicated to transport multiple atoms and to correctly rearrange them on the far end of your teleporter. Keep in mind that the average human body comprises 7×10^{27} atoms, and you get the idea that nobody is traveling by teleporter any time soon.

TRUE OR FALSE? Time travel is possible with today's technology.

TRUE.

You do it all the time, traveling through space as time moves forward.

TRUE OR FALSE? Time travel to the *distant* future is possible with today's technology.

TRUE.

But it's another trick question. The faster you travel, the slower time passes for you relative to external observers. Which means an astronaut returning to Earth is a few milliseconds younger than his or her friends left behind. If you left Earth at age 20 and traveled for five years at 99.5 percent of the speed of light, you would return to Earth at age 25 and your friends would be 70. So in that sense, time travel to the future is definitely possible.

TRUE OR FALSE? Time travel to the past is possible with today's technology.

NOT SURE.

Probably not, and best not to ask unless you want your head to explode when your future self travels back in time and steals your wallet.

TRUE OR FALSE? Gravity is caused by a warping of space and time.

TRUE.

At least that's the way Albert Einstein explained it in his *General Theory of Relativity*. Isaac Newton developed the first model of gravity, suggesting that gravity is a force of attraction that exists between any two objects. But Newton's theories are not able to describe why light bends when passing near massive objects such as the sun, or why clocks in space speed up relative to clocks on Earth. Thank Einstein for these latter two insights.

TRUE OR FALSE? Besides formulating the laws of gravity, Isaac Newton is generally credited with inventing the cat door.

LIKELY TRUE.

Chaucer may have described the first cat-flap-like contrivance fitted on a door, but contemporaries credit Sir Isaac Newton with having carved holes in his door for the "egress of cat and kitten."

TRUE OR FALSE? Time has not always existed.

TRUE.

According to Einstein's general theory of relativity, neither space nor time existed prior to the Big Bang some 13.7 billion years ago. Before the Big Bang, everything—including time—was packed together into an extremely tiny dot.

TRUE OR FALSE? En route to their historic moon landing, Apollo 11 astronauts Neil Armstrong, Buzz Aldrin, and Michael Collins ate bacon squares, peaches, cream of chicken soup, and date fruitcake.

TRUE.

TRUE OR FALSE? Astronauts shrink up to 2 inches when they return to Earth after a mission in space.

TRUE.

The diminished gravity in space means astronauts typically "grow" a few inches as their vertebrae expand as they leave Earth's orbit. The effect is reversed when they return to Earth.

TRUE OR FALSE? A sand wedge is the only golf club to have been used on the moon.

FALSE.

It was an 8-iron, struck by Alan Sheppard on the Apollo 14 mission. He hit three golf balls in total.

TRUE OR FALSE? "Ten elite brains" is an anagram of Albert Einstein.

TRUE.

So, too, are "tiniest enabler" and "Leninist beater."

TRUE OR FALSE? Albert Einstein flunked math.

FALSE.

That's just a rumor propagated by people who don't like math.

The Speed of Light

Light travels at 300,000 kilometers per second. On the open highway, that's just 1 billion kilometers per hour. A light year is the distance light travels in one year, roughly 9,461 billion kilometers. If you're curious, here are times it takes light to travel:

- From the moon to Earth: 1.3 seconds

- From the sun to Earth: 8.5 minutes

- From the nearest solar system to Earth: 4.3 years

- From the nearest galaxy beyond the Milky Way to Earth: 2.5 million years

- From the edge of the observable universe to Earth: 78 billion years

TRUE OR FALSE? Upon their return to Earth, Apollo 11 astronauts were kept in quarantine for twenty-one days to prevent any harmful lunar bacteria or other organisms from infecting the planet.

TRUE.

NASA kept the quarantine in place for all returning astronauts until 1977.

TRUE OR FALSE? To escape Earth's gravity, spaceships leaving the planet must travel at a minimum of 25,000 miles per hour.

TRUE.

That's known as Earth's escape velocity. The average flight into orbit takes about eight and a half minutes.

TRUE OR FALSE? Only five manmade objects have left the solar system.

TRUE.

The *Voyager 1* space probe is the farthest out, having crossed into deep space in 2012. The other crafts to have escaped the solar system are *Pioneer 10* and *11*, *Voyager 2*, and the *New Horizons* spacecraft.

TRUE OR FALSE? No stars will actually collide when the Milky Way and Andromeda galaxies collide in roughly 4 billion years.

TRUE.

The odds of any two stars actually colliding are exceedingly small, considering the large distances separating them. Think of it this way: if our solar system was a coin, the nearest solar system to us would be another coin placed more than 200 yards away when the two galaxies collide.

Did you know?

The observable universe has more than 10 billion trillion stars arranged in about 100 billion galaxies. It's roughly 156 billion light years across. Just don't ask what's on the other side.

And don't ask where we are in the universe. All we know is that we are at the center of the part we can see.

TRUE OR FALSE? The universe is flat.

TRUE.

Being flat means the universe is likely infinite too. Which is good news. It means we will not eventually die in the so-called "Big Crunch"—when all matter in the universe collapses in on itself and we die, followed by another Big Bang. At least that's what scientists now believe. Hooray for flat universes!

TRUE OR FALSE? In the hope of attracting alien life in distant galaxies, scientists on Earth beamed ten thousand Twitter messages into space using a high-energy transmitter.

TRUE.

It's unclear if aliens care much about earthly celebrities and trending topics on Twitter.

TRUE OR FALSE? NASA sent golden records into space in 1977 with the *Voyager 1* and *2* spacecraft, so that aliens can rock out to Peruvian panpipes and Chuck Berry's "Johnny B. Goode."

TRUE.

The records were the idea of Carl Sagan, who led the committee that decided what should be included on the records. Besides Chuck Berry and Peruvian panpipes, there are tracks from Bach, Mozart, and Beethoven; sounds from Earth; and recordings of people saying "hello" in dozens of languages. The idea is that some future interstellar civilization will find the records and figure out how to play them.

Did you know?

President Jimmy Carter included a note on the *Voyager* golden records that ends with the less-than-optimistic line: "We are attempting to survive our time so we may live into yours."

Sheesh Jimmy, where's your optimism? Turn the thermostat down and put your sweater back on.

TRUE OR FALSE? If you hold up a grain of sand and look at it against the night sky, the patch of sky it obscures contains five thousand galaxies.

FALSE.

The patch of sky the sand obscures is actually home to roughly ten thousand galaxies.

TRUE OR FALSE? About 95 percent of the universe is missing.

____
TRUE.

Not quite 5 percent of the universe's matter and energy is what scientists call "ordinary" matter—you, me, your cat, plus anything and everything in our universe, including every atom and electron and Higgs boson in existence. All of this adds up to 4.9 percent of the amount of matter and energy that physicists say *should* exist in the universe. What about the other 95.1 percent? Apparently it's a mixture of dark matter and dark energy, which neither react with light nor ever have been detected or measured. It's a little creepy that we don't understand where 95.1 percent of our universe is hiding.

TRUE OR FALSE? X-rays are named after their inventor, Doctor X.

____
FALSE.

When X-rays were invented in 1895, scientists did not understand how these waves of electromagnetic radiation worked or whether they were harmful. So they were named "X-radiation" after the X variable in algebra, which always represents the unknown. Calling them "Röntgen rays" after their inventor, Wilhelm Röntgen, never caught on, at least not in English-speaking countries.

TRUE OR FALSE? The original goal of radar was to generate a "death ray" that could destroy enemy aircraft.

____
TRUE.

Radar, an acronym for "*RAdio Detection And Ranging*," is now used to detect objects in the sky, on land, or on the surface of the ocean. It was originally conceived by the British government in the 1930s, however, as means of incinerating enemy aircraft before they could bomb the British homeland. Tests proved death rays were unfeasible, so the British transformed the technology into an early-warning air-defense system.

Which of the following futuristic technologies does *not* exist?

1 Self-healing airplanes. The idea is simple: infuse metals with the ability to "remember" shapes, so that subsequent dents and tears are instantly fixed as the metal returns to its originally specified shape. It's made possible by electrically charging the metals to be shape memorizing.

2 Meshworms. These tiny robots are the size of your thumb and made of soft, highly durable synthetic material. They move using the process of peristalsis to contract parts of their bodies and push themselves forward, like earthworms. Meshworms are virtually indestructible and will continue to operate even if you smack them with a sledgehammer. No surprise—the military wants to use meshworms as small, silent spies that can go safely where human soldiers cannot.

3 Flying cars. *Terrafugia's Transition* is a propeller-driven airplane that, upon landing, transforms itself into a car that you can legally drive on the freeway at speeds up to 65 miles per hour. The company calls it a street-legal airplane and has a long list of enthusiasts who've signed up to pay upward of $200,000 for the first fly-drive vehicles.

4 Hover boards. Or more accurately, HUVr boards. The company HUVr has designed a hover board similar to a skateboard that allows users to levitate 6 to 10 inches above the ground and move forward, backward, and side to side at the pace of a brisk walk. The boards can be activated via Bluetooth. Smartphone apps are used to track route details such as distance and travel time.

5 Liquid body armor. Mix cornstarch and water slowly and nothing happens; speed up your stirring, and the mixture turns thick and resistant. This same concept applies to dampening the impact of a bullet or piece of shrapnel when a similarly "shear-thickening" substance is woven into a fabric. Early versions of the armor are 2.5 times more effective than the current best-in-class material, Kevlar.

6 Invisible tanks. The British army is testing the concept of making its tanks and armored vehicles invisible. They do it by filming the surroundings in real time and projecting the image back onto tanks and vehicles covered in a reflective material. The effect makes the tanks fade completely into the environment (at least visually—you can, of course, still hear them).

ANSWER

4 Despite a very cool website and celebrity endorsements by the likes of skateboarder Tony Hawk and musician Moby, HUVr boards remain an awesome viral hoax.

TRUE OR FALSE? The U.S. Navy has a microwave ray gun that beams sounds directly into human skulls.

_____
TRUE.

The Navy calls it MEDUSA (Mob Excess Deterrent Using Silent Audio) and uses it for crowd control, among other undisclosed and classified applications. The gun shoots a microwave that enters the head and can be detected by the ears; since the sound does not come through the ears, however, it can be much louder—to the point where it could knock you out cold.

TRUE OR FALSE? Glass is a solid.

_____
FALSE.

Glass is a liquid, albeit a very slow-moving liquid.

TRUE OR FALSE? A ball of glass will bounce higher than a ball of rubber.

_____
TRUE.

Bouncing has everything to do with how much energy is lost when your ball collides with a surface. Rubber deforms easily and loses a fair amount of its energy to the collision surface. A glass ball, however, is stiff and loses much less energy to a solid surface. Which means it will bounce higher as long as you don't drop it from a height that will make the glass ball shatter.

TRUE OR FALSE? A bucket of water contains more atoms than there are buckets of water on the surface of Earth.

_____
FALSE.

A one-gallon bucket contains roughly 1.264×10^{26} atoms of water. All the water on earth (fresh and salt) contains roughly 1.385×10^{48} atoms.

TRUE OR FALSE? About half the water on Earth is salt water, and the other half is freshwater.

FALSE.

Only 3 percent of Earth's water is freshwater. The other 97 percent is salt water.

TRUE OR FALSE? All the rivers, lakes, swamps, and ponds on Earth comprise just 0.3 percent of the planet's freshwater supply.

TRUE.

Most freshwater on Earth is frozen in glaciers or stored deep underground.

TRUE OR FALSE? The atmosphere contains more freshwater than all the rivers on Earth combined.

TRUE.

A vast amount of freshwater—enough to cover the entire surface of Earth an inch deep in rain—is stored in the atmosphere.

TRUE OR FALSE? Water is the only substance on Earth naturally found in liquid, gaseous, and solid states.

TRUE.

TRUE OR FALSE? One inch of rain is equivalent to 10 inches of snow.

TRUE.

With a caveat. One inch of rain will generate about 10 inches of snow at temperatures around 30 degrees. In colder weather, more snow is likely to be generated per inch of rain. On the flip side, you'll get less snow from an inch of rain when it's slushy and wet, or mixed with freezing rain.

A 1 month

B 7 years

C 20½ years

D 29 years

ANSWER

C. The average American uses 100 gallons of water per day. More than 750,000 gallons of water flows over Niagara Falls each second.

TRUE OR FALSE? There's more liquid water on Jupiter's moon Europa than there is on Earth.

TRUE.

While it has not been proved beyond a doubt, NASA estimates that Europa's oceans contain twice as much water as there is on the surface of Earth. Not bad for a moon that's roughly the same size as Earth's own moon.

TRUE OR FALSE? The largest snowflakes ever recorded measured more than 15 inches across.

TRUE.

The *Guinness Book of World Records* lists snowflakes from an 1887 snowstorm in Montana as measuring 15 inches . . . yes, inches.

1	New automobile	A	10 gallons
2	Slice of bread	B	1,000 gallons
3	Cotton T-shirt	C	634 gallons
4	1 gallon of milk	D	713 gallons
5	1 hamburger	E	9,090 gallons

ANSWERS

1E, 2A, 3D, 4B, 5C

TRUE OR FALSE? Snow is not white.

TRUE.

Visible light is white. Snow crystals are clear and do not absorb visible light, but instead reflect it back evenly. Snow appears white because it does not absorb any light.

TRUE OR FALSE? Eskimos have more than one hundred words for snow and its variants.

FALSE.

Eskimo-Aleut languages have roughly the same number of words for snow as does English.

FOOD

DRINK

. CHAPTER 2 .

Food & Drink

TRUE OR FALSE? Honey is the only food produced by an insect that humans eat.

TRUE.

TRUE OR FALSE? To make one pound of honey, bees must tap an average of 2 million flowers and fly more than fifty thousand miles.

TRUE.

More impressive still: A single honeybee produces a scant 1/12th teaspoon of honey in its lifetime.

TRUE OR FALSE? Honey is the only natural food that does not rot.

TRUE.

In theory, a jar of honey could sit for a million years and remain completely edible.

TRUE OR FALSE? You could live your entire life eating nothing but honey.

__
TRUE.

Honey contains sugar (80 percent) and water (20 percent) and is the only complete food in nature. If necessary you could survive on a diet of pure honey (never mind your teeth).

TRUE OR FALSE? Lemons contain more sugar than strawberries.

__
TRUE.

TRUE OR FALSE? Strawberries are the only fruits with seeds on the outside.

__
TRUE.

 **Did you know?**

Native Americans introduced strawberries to early European settlers. The berries were crushed, mixed with cornmeal, and baked into bread. *Et voila!* Meet the strawberry shortcake.

TRUE OR FALSE? Strawberries continue to ripen after being picked.

__
TRUE.

It's the same with apples. Oranges, though, do not.

TRUE OR FALSE? Apples ripen faster if they are refrigerated.

FALSE.

Most fruit, including apples, ripens fastest at room temperature.

TRUE OR FALSE? Apples are the most popular fruit in the U.S.

TRUE.

TRUE OR FALSE? Grapes explode when you put them in the microwave.

TRUE.

And our apologies if you have young kids, grapes, and a microwave.

TRUE OR FALSE? Navel oranges get their name from the belly-button-shaped nub opposite the stem.

TRUE.

The larger the orange's navel, the sweeter the orange is.

TRUE OR FALSE? In ancient times oranges—not apples— were known as the "fruits of the Gods."

TRUE.

In fact, oranges and not apples are the so-called "golden apples" stolen by Hercules. Go figure.

TRUE OR FALSE? The ancient Egyptians ate bananas.

TRUE.

Hieroglyphs depict Egyptians from three thousand years ago eating bananas.

TRUE OR FALSE? Banana trees are not trees.

__True.__

They are not trees; they are giant herbaceous plants. To qualify as trees, banana stems would need to contain true woody tissue.

➤ **EVER WONDER HOW YOUR FAVORITE FRUITS AND VEGE-TABLES ARE RELATED? FOR EACH FRUIT OR VEGETABLE IN THE FIRST COLUMN, PICK A FRUIT OR VEGETABLE IN THE SECOND COLUMN THAT SHARES THE SAME BOTANICAL CLASSIFICATION.**

1	Almond	A	Peanut
2	Cauliflower	B	Spinach
3	Pea	C	Mustard
4	Tomato	D	Potato
5	Beet	E	Lettuce
6	Sunflower	F	Peach
7	Carrot	G	Cilantro
8	Garlic	H	Basil
9	Mint	I	Buckwheat
10	Rhubarb	J	Onion

ANSWERS

1F, 2C, 3A, 4D, 5B, 6E, 7G, 8J, 9H, 10I

TRUE OR FALSE? Worcestershire sauce is created by dissolving whole anchovies in vinegar, until the bones melt.

__True.__

TRUE OR FALSE? The original five Campbell's Soup flavors were tomato, consommé, vegetable, chicken, and oxtail.

TRUE.

TRUE OR FALSE? Scotland's national dish, haggis, is made by boiling the heart, liver, lungs, and small intestine of a calf or sheep in its own stomach, then seasoning with onions, oatmeal, and suet.

TRUE.

It's just one of those things you have to try—words don't do it justice.

TRUE OR FALSE? A single hamburger from a fast-food chain can contain meat from more than ten different cows.

FALSE.

It can actually contain meat from more than *a hundred* different cows.

TRUE OR FALSE? Some fast-food hamburgers are made of only 12 percent meat.

TRUE.

The, um, remainders are water, bone, cartilage, plant material, and—yummy!—parasites.

TRUE OR FALSE? More than 45 percent of Americans eat fast food once a week.

TRUE.

And a dispiriting 22 percent of Americans think fast food is good for you.

TRUE OR FALSE? McDonald's earns the majority of its profits from collecting rents, not from selling food.

TRUE.

TRUE OR FALSE? Each day McDonald's feeds more people than the entire population of Spain.

TRUE.

That's more than 47 million people served each and every day at the Golden Arches.

TRUE OR FALSE? To burn the calories consumed eating a McDonald's Big Mac, large fries, and a large soda, you must walk briskly for 50 hours straight.

FALSE.

It's not quite as bad as that. You'll only need to walk briskly nonstop for seven straight hours.

TRUE OR FALSE? The eggs at some national fast-food chains contain solvents and antifoaming agents.

TRUE.

It's actually *worse* than you think. These "eggs" include not just glycerin (solvent) and dimethylpolysiloxane (antifoaming agent) but also propylene glycol, a preservative used in tobacco and electronic cigarettes.

TRUE OR FALSE? If you've eaten at McDonald's, you've likely eaten a goopy paste created when the bones and carcass of leftover chickens are combined in a food processor.

FALSE.

It's called "mechanically separated chicken," and after an uproar in 2014, McDonald's vehemently denied using the goop in its signature Chicken McNuggets. The company released a video that showed how its McNuggets are actually made—while the process is not pretty, there is no pink slime.

Geography of the Obese

Are Americans really that fat? Test your knowledge by ranking the following countries based on their average daily intake of calories, from most gluttonous to underfed:

- Australia
- Austria
- Canada
- Cuba
- Eritrea
- Greece
- Italy
- Romania
- United Kingdom
- United States

ANSWER

United States, Austria, Greece, Italy, Canada, Romania, United Kingdom, Cuba, Australia, Eritrea. So yeah, Americans really are that fat.

TRUE OR FALSE? Due to concerns over mad cow disease, the U.S. Department of Agriculture ruled in 2004 that mechanically separated beef is prohibited for use as human food.

TRUE.

Did you know?

Since 1996, the U.S. Department of Agriculture has required mechanically separated poultry and pork to be labeled as such in ingredient lists. Just don't serve mechanically separated beef to customers—that's a felony.

TRUE OR FALSE? The U.S. Food and Drug Administration allows pizza sauce at fast-food restaurants to contain a maximum of thirty fly eggs per 100 grams, or fifteen fly eggs and one maggot per 100 grams, or two maggots per 100 grams.

TRUE.

Bon appetit!

TRUE OR FALSE? When Heinz ketchup leaves the bottle, it travels at a rate of .028 miles per hour, or thirty-five miles per year.

TRUE.

And it's probably why Heinz chose the Carly Simon song "Anticipation" as the soundtrack for its television commercials in the 1970s and '80s.

Witch's Brew: Hair of Rodent, Fragment of Insect

The good news? The U.S. Food and Drug Administration (FDA) regulates the amount of mold, wormy bits, and insect parts that our food may contain.

The bad news? The FDA allows mold, wormy bits, and insect parts into our food in the first place!

Here are the established maximum levels of contamination allowed by the FDA:

- Frozen peaches may contain up to 3 percent wormy or moldy fruit.

- Canned pineapple cannot contain more than 20 percent moldy fruit pieces.

- No more than two rodent hairs, or twenty gnawed kernels, can be shipped in a pound of popcorn.

- Chocolate must contain fewer than sixty insect fragments per 100 grams, and no more than one rodent hair.

- Shelled peanuts must have fewer than twenty whole insects in a 100-pound bag.

- Ground pepper must contain fewer than 475 insect fragments per 50 grams.

TRUE OR FALSE? The best spot to tap on a bottle of Heinz ketchup is the "57" label on the neck.

TRUE.

Tap firmly where the bottle narrows and the ketchup will flow, according to the official Heinz website.

 **Did you know?**

The upside-down ketchup bottle was the brainchild of inventor Paul Brown, who spent years developing a valve that would open when an inverted bottle was squeezed and then close automatically without leaking. Now Brown's patented valve is used by NASA (so that astronauts' cups don't spill) and by baby food and shampoo makers.

TRUE OR FALSE? Ketchup is normally thick like honey, but becomes thin and flows like water when shaken or stirred.

TRUE.

Ketchup is a complex fluid prone to "shear thinning"—which means it flows when disturbed but is otherwise thick and viscous.

TRUE OR FALSE? The French government banned ketchup in its primary schools in 2011, fearing it encourages children to develop Americanized taste preferences.

TRUE.

Go squeeze an extra helping of ketchup on your freedom fries, America!

TRUE OR FALSE? In China, the most popular use of ketchup is as a condiment for fried chicken.

TRUE.

In the United States the most popular uses for ketchup are as a condiment for hamburgers, hot dogs, and French fries. The Swedes use it as a topping on pasta. In Romania, it's a popular pizza topping.

TRUE OR FALSE? The idea of eating beans on toast was invented in 1927 by the Heinz company.

TRUE.

It also popularized the idea of eating beans for breakfast.

TRUE OR FALSE? There is no difference between "ketchup" and "catsup" other than the spelling.

TRUE.

TRUE OR FALSE? Tomatoes are a fruit, not a vegetable.

TRUE.

Most Americans wrongly believed, until the late 18th century, that tomatoes were poisonous. Former president Ronald Reagan wrongly believed that tomatoes were a vegetable.

TRUE OR FALSE? The ice cream chain Baskin-Robins once tested the flavors ketchup, lox and bagels, and grape Britain.

TRUE.

Though tested, the flavors were never widely released. Two scoops of vanilla and ketchup, anybody?

TRUE OR FALSE? Vanilla is the most popular flavor of ice cream sold in the United States.

TRUE.

Chocolate is a distant second.

TRUE OR FALSE? Alaskans eat twice as much ice cream as the average American.

TRUE.

That's saying something, since the average American consumes a whopping 48 pints each year.

TRUE OR FALSE? Former President Ronald Reagan is responsible for designating a National Ice Cream Month and a National Ice Cream Day.

TRUE.

National Ice Cream Month is celebrated in July, and the third Sunday in July is officially National Ice Cream Day.

⤞⤞⤞⤞⤞⤞⤞ **Did you know?** ⤝⤝⤝⤝⤝⤝⤝

"Brain freeze" happens when something cold, such as ice cream, touches the roof of your mouth and causes blood vessels in your head to dilate.

Q What is the top-selling candy in the United States?

A M&Ms. The candy was invented in 1941 and named after its two inventors, Forrest E. Mars and R. Bruce Murrie. Peanut M&Ms debuted in 1954.

Q What is the second-most popular candy in the United States?

A Reese's Peanut Butter Cups, invented in 1923 by a former Hershey's chocolate employee.

Q What's the third-most popular candy in the United States?

A The Snickers bar. It was the second candy bar developed by the Mars family. It hit the shelves in 1930 and was named after one of the family's horses.

Q When were gummy bears invented?

A 1922, by the German candy company Haribo. The first gummy was called the Dancing Bear, predecessor to today's Gold-Bear.

Q Haribo's 1930 companion to the Dancing Bear, the Teddy Bear, was named after whom?

A U.S. President Theodore Roosevelt, who was an avid bear hunter.

Q What does Haribo's official slogan—*Haribo macht Kinder froh*—mean?

A "Haribo makes children happy."

Q How many gummy bears does the Haribo company produce each day?

A Roughly 100 million. If all the Haribo gummy bears produced in a year were laid head to paw they would circle the earth four times.

Each year Americans spend $9 billion on candy and consume more than 25 pounds per person.

Q What is the Number 1 candy-related search term on the Yahoo! website?

A Candy corn.

Q What corn-related food did the Pilgrims eat at America's first Thanksgiving celebration?

A Popcorn.

⇛ HOW MUCH DOES MOVIE THEATER POPCORN COST TO MAKE?

A 1 cent per ounce

B 5 cents per ounce

C 10 cents per ounce

D 25 cents per ounce

ANSWER

C. It's not a healthy snack, but it's certainly healthy for the bottom line: Movie theaters sell popcorn for more than it costs to buy filet mignon, ounce for ounce.

Q How many calories are in a large movie-theater popcorn?

A More than 1,200 calories if you include the "butter" topping. That's the equivalent of the calories in one pound of baby back ribs or two McDonald's Big Macs.

Q For each dollar spent at a movie theater's concession stands, how much is pure profit?

A Roughly 85 cents.

➤ HOW MANY CALORIES DOES EACH OF THE FOLLOWING FOOD ITEMS CONTAIN?

1	McDonald's Big Mac	A	285 calories
2	Bagel and cream cheese	B	105 calories
3	20 oz. bottle of Coca-Cola	C	42 calories
4	Slice of cheese pizza	D	550 calories
5	12 oz. bottle of beer	E	155 calories
6	Banana	F	400 calories
7	Snicker's bar	G	98 calories
8	Shot of 80-proof whiskey	H	233 calories
9	Cup of coffee with whole milk	I	554 calories

ANSWERS
1D, 2F, 3H, 4A, 5E, 6B, 7I, 8G, 9C

Accidental Foods

- **Corn flakes.** Corn flakes were invented by Seventh Day Adventists looking for wholesome vegetarian food to feed patients at a sanitarium in Michigan. The Kellogg brothers stumbled upon a process of boiling, drying, and toasting oats and corn purely by accident. They started with a bowl of stale boiled oats and, instead of tossing them out, decided to roll them out like dough. These turned into flakes that, when toasted, provided a healthy and delicious meal to patients. In 1906, the brothers founded the Kellogg's company to sell their new invention.

- **Chocolate chip cookies.** Chocolate chip cookies were invented at the Toll House Inn in 1930, when Martha Wakefield substituted fragments of sweetened chocolate in her chocolate-cookie batter. She assumed the chocolate would simply melt into the dough and was surprised when it didn't. Today Toll House Cookies are the most popular cookies in the United States.

- **Nachos.** Ignacio Anaya was the chef at a restaurant called the Victory Club in Piedras Negras, Mexico, just across the border from Texas. One day in 1943, when his kitchen was short of ingredients, he served a plate of fried tortilla chips, melted cheese, and jalepeño peppers to a group of Texas women on a shopping trip. He called them nachos especiale and the name stuck.

- **Potato chips.** It's said the first potato chips were invented accidentally in 1853 at a resort near Saratoga Springs, New York. When a customer repeatedly complained about the sogginess of the establishment's fried potatoes, the chef reportedly sliced the potatoes paper-thin and fried them in grease in an attempt to make them inedible. Of course the customer loved them, and "Saratoga Chips" became an overnight sensation throughout New England.

- **Sandwiches.** Sandwiches were invented quite accidentally in the 1740s by John Montagu, the fourth Earl of Sandwich. At the gaming tables the earl would order sliced meat in between slices of bread. The idea caught on and was popularized under the name "sandwich."

- **Coca-Cola.** The original recipe for Coca-Cola was invented in 1866 by John Pemberton, a pharmacist and former Confederate soldier addicted to morphine. Pemberton created many tonics that he hoped would help kick his morphine addiction; one concoction featured cocaine (legal at the time) and the highly caffeinated kola nut. Poor, strung out, and on his deathbed, Pemberton sold the recipe in 1888 to Asa Candler, the co-founder of Coca-Cola. Candler paid $550 for the recipe that would turn Coca-Cola into the U.S.'s most popular soda.

Q Which makes you more intoxicated, drinking cocktails with regular soda or cocktails with diet soda?

A Cocktails with diet soda. They get you more drunk, more quickly, than regular sodas, because artificial sweeteners speed alcohol absorption.

➤ WHICH COUNTRIES DRINK THE MOST BEER EACH YEAR, ON A PER-CAPITA BASIS? TEST YOUR BEER KNOWLEDGE BY MATCHING COUNTRY WITH CONSUMPTION.

1	Germany	A	132 liters
2	Austria	B	107 liters
3	Australia	C	106 liters
4	Czech Republic	D	104 liters
5	Canada	E	98 liters
6	Ireland	F	96 liters

ANSWERS
1B, 2C, 3F, 4A, 5E, 6D

Q How much beer do Americans drink each year?

A 78 liters per person. That's roughly nine hundred and thirty-six 12-ounce bottles per person, or roughly two and a half bottles of beer per day for every man, woman, and child in the country. While that sounds like a lot of beer, Americans rank just thirteenth on the list of global consumption.

Q What is the most popular alcohol in South Korea?

A Soju. It's a fermented rice spirit that accounts for 97 percent of the South Korean alcohol market.

Q What country drinks the most wine annually?

A Vatican City. Residents of the Holy See consume double the number of bottles per year drunk in France or Italy as a whole.

Q What countries occupy the second and third slots on the list of per-capita wine consumers?

A Andorra and Luxembourg, at fifty and forty-nine liters per capita, respectively. Apparently, in small countries it's easier to consume copious amounts of wine.

Q How much wine do the French drink each year?

A 45.6 liters per person, earning the Number Four spot on the global list of wine consumers.

Q How much wine do Americans consume each year?

A A teetotaling 10 liters per person, for sixty-second place. At sixty-first place among the world's wine consumers is the Netherland Antilles. This is likely the only time Netherland Antilles outranks the United States on *any* list.

Q What country is the world's largest daily consumer of coffee?

A The Netherlands, which consumes a whopping 2.4 cups per person, per day. The United States ranks a measly sixteenth on the list: As a nation, we don't drink even one cup a day! Shame on us and our paltry 0.93 cups per day.

Culinary Heroes

Q

Which of the following culinary heroes and heroines are real and which are fictional?

1 Baby Ruth

5 Colonel Sanders

2 Betty Crocker

6 Granny Smith

3 Cap'n Crunch

7 Orville Redenbacher

4 Chef Boyardee

8 Sara Lee

ANSWERS

1 Half real. Baby Ruth is a famous chocolate bar invented in 1921 by the Curtiss Candy Company in Chicago. The company has always claimed Baby Ruth was named after President Cleveland's first daughter, Ruth Cleveland—and not after baseball icon George Herman "Babe" Ruth. Unfortunately for the truth, Ruth Cleveland died of diphtheria in 1904; George Herman became a famous baseball star in 1920 and '21, just as the candy bar was introduced. So we'll score this as half fake—the candy bar is named after a real person, just not the person claimed by the company itself. Blame the lawyers (the Curtiss Candy Company fought several lawsuits over this issue).

2   Fake. Yes, Betty Crocker is as fake as a $3 bill. The name was invented in 1921 to deal with a flood of customer letters about a promotion sponsored by the General Mills company. The name combines the last name of a retiring company executive (William Crocker) with the "friendly sounding" name Betty.

3   Fake. The Cap'n and his crew were created in 1963 by Jay Ward, a well-known producer of animated television cartoons. He's credited with Rocky & Bullwinkle, Dudley Do-Right, George of the Jungle, Tom Slick, and Super Chicken, to name just a few.

4   Real. Chef Boyardee is the man behind canned Beefaroni, beef ravioli, and spaghetti and meatballs. The real-life inspiration was born Ettore (Hector) Boiardi in northern Italy in 1898. He arrived in New York in 1915 and began cooking at the prestigious Plaza Hotel. He later moved to Cleveland and opened his own restaurant, Il Giardino d'Italia. He later changed his name to the easier-to-pronounce "Boyardee" and began selling his famous spaghetti in cans. Despite his company being purchased by American Home Foods (now part of ConAgra), Chef Boyardee worked in the kitchens until his death in 1987.

5   Real. Colonel Sanders was born Harlan Sanders in Henryville, Indiana, in 1890. According to his official autobiography he was a "sixth-grade dropout, a farmhand, an army mule-tender, a locomotive fireman, a railroad worker, an aspiring lawyer, an insurance salesman, a ferryboat entrepreneur, a tire salesman, an amateur

obstetrician, an (unsuccessful) political candidate, a gas station operator, a motel operator, and finally, a restaurateur." What makes his story interesting is that he didn't start his first fried-chicken business in Kentucky until the tender age of 65. By 1963, he had more than 500 franchises operating around the U.S.

6   Real. This famous breed of apple is named after real-life Mary Ann Smith, an Australian homemaker. Smith discovered the original trees in her home orchard; the fruit was tart and stayed firm in her pies. The fruit caught on and was widely marketed in both Australia and the United States. The name Granny Smith stuck.

7   Real. Orville Redenbacher is as real as they come. Born in Indiana corn country in 1907, Orville dedicated most of his life to popcorn. In 1969, he marketed a new strain of corn that popped incredibly efficiently, with a 44:1 ratio of popped to unpopped kernels. Orville skyrocketed to fame with his first television commercial in 1976, which ended with the now-famous line, "You'll like it better or my name isn't Orville Redenbacher."

8   Real. There is a real Sara Lee: she was the 8-year-old daughter of Charles Lubin, who launched the company in 1949 with a popular cream cheesecake. The name of the company was officially the Kitchens of Sara Lee. In 1953, Lubin was the first to mass-market frozen desserts that could be shipped cross-country. Fame and fortune followed.

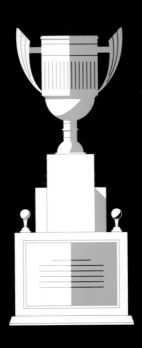

SPORTS

• CHAPTER 3 •

Sports

Q What sport features famous characters such as Anger Management, King Kong, Big Dawg, Dragon Slayer, and El Loco Hombre?

A Monster truck racing.

Q What sport's most famous competitions include the Daytona 500, the Coca-Cola 600, and the Brickyard 400?

A The National Association for Stock Car Auto Racing (NASCAR). Aggressive television distribution has elevated stock car racing to the second-most watched sport in America (behind football). The average top speeds at NASCAR stock events are an eye-popping 190 to 200 miles per hour.

Q What sport has no goalkeepers and no fixed positions, and has players who wear neither helmets nor protective padding and who move the ball by kicking or running with it, or by passing it in any direction with an open-hand tap—or by punching it with a closed fist?

A Australian Rules Football. Go Aussie!

Q What sport has been banned by public schools in six U.S. states?

A Dodgeball.

Q When was the first recorded game of handball played?

A 1427. That's the first written mention of a game involving a ball being hit by hand against a wall. Apparently King James I of England requested a palace wall to be filled in, to improve the playing surface. The modern game was codified in Denmark in the 1900s. It's been played continuously at the Olympics since 1972 (it was a demonstration sport at the 1936 and 1952 Olympic games).

Q What two sports were invented days apart in 1891 at the very same place in Massachusetts?

A Netball and basketball.

Q What were used for baskets in the very first games of basketball?

A Peach baskets. The sport's inventor, James Naismith, was looking for a way to entertain a group of boys inside a gym at a YMCA in Massachusetts. He hammered a peach basket to the wall about 10 feet off the ground and—voilà! Basketball was born.

Q What were the very first balls used in basketball?

A Soccer balls, which are not famous for their bouncing qualities. As a result, passing and running—not dribbling—dominated the early game. In fact, dribbling didn't become important in basketball until the early 1950s, when the modern (and fully round—duh!) basketball was introduced.

Worldwide, more than 20 million people regularly play netball, which makes it one of the most famous sports Americans have never heard of. It's ironic given that netball was created in America, by Americans, specifically to be a less physical version of the iconic American sport of basketball.

Q Who is the tallest player ever in the National Basketball Association (NBA)?

A It's a two-way tie for first place. Manute Bol from Sudan and Gheorghe Muresan from Romania top the NBA charts at 7 feet, 7 inches. Bol played for the Washington Bullets (today's Wizards) and Philadelphia 76ers, Muresan for the Bullets and New Jersey Nets. Despite their height advantage, neither player had stellar NBA careers, due to frequent injuries.

Q Who is the shortest NBA player ever?

A Tyrone Bogues. The famous "little giant" stood 5 feet, 3 inches. During a ten-year career with the Charlotte Hornets he proved that speed and agility—not just height—matter on the court.

Q Who is the top NBA scorer of all time?

A Kareem Abdul-Jabbar. The Los Angeles Lakers' forward had a twenty-year career total of 38,387 points. Karl Malone comes in second with 36,928 points, Michael Jordan in third with 32,292.

Q How long has basketball been a full-medal sport at the Olympics?

A Since the Munich Olympics in 1936. Interestingly, the sport's governing body dropped the distinction between amateurs and professionals in 1989 (highly controversial in some quarters). This has allowed professional American basketball players to compete at the Olympics since 1992. Women's basketball was added to the Olympics in 1976.

 **Did you know?**

Women have played basketball from the sport's earliest days; the first intercollegiate women's basketball game, between Stanford and UC Berkeley, was played in 1896.

Stanford won.

Q Where was volleyball invented?

A Massachusetts. Yes—the same U.S. state where basketball and netball were invented. Volleyball was the brainchild of William Morgan, who, in 1895, blended tennis and handball into a less physical sport than the newly popular (and physically rougher) sport of basketball.

Q Where was beach volleyball invented?

A Santa Monica, California. The first official set of beach volleyball was played in 1950; it's been an Olympic sport continuously since 1996.

Q What is the only official clothing players are allowed to wear during a match of beach volleyball?

A Swimsuit, plus an optional hat. Those are the rules according to the Fédération Internationale de Volleyball (FIVB), the sport's international governing body.

Did you know?

After soccer, volleyball is the world's second most-played sport. An estimated 46 million Americans, and more than 800 million people worldwide, play volleyball at least weekly.

Q What's the original name of the sport most Americans call soccer?

A Association football. The rules of the sport were first codified in the 1860s by the Football Association (FA) in England. Even at the international level, the sport's global governing body is the eponymous Fédération Internationale de Football Association (FIFA). Clearly the name "association football" has a long and glorious history.

Q What does "FC" stand for in the names of Major League Soccer (MLS) teams FC Dallas, Seattle Sounders FC, and Vancouver Whitecaps FC?

A Football Club.

Q Where does the name "soccer" come from?

A The British invented the word "soccer" in the 1890s—it's originally an abbreviation of the word "association," as in "assoc." Don't listen to naysayers who claim the word "soccer" is an abomination: For most of the twentieth century, the sport was known interchangeably as soccer or football.

POP QUIZ

Name that Famous Soccer Player

Think you know soccer? Prove it by identifying the following seven players.

1 Scored 49 international goals for England and played for seventeen seasons with Manchester United.

2 Played for Moscow Dynamo in the Soviet Super League and saved a miraculous 150 penalty shots over his career. The only Soviet player ever named European Player of the Year.

3 At the tender age of 17, scored six goals at the 1958 World Cup leading Brazil to its first title.

4 Led France to victory at the 1998 World Cup and Euro 2000, in addition to helping his team, Real Madrid, win the 2002 UEFA Champions League. He is one of just 2 three-time FIFA World Player of the Year winners.

5 Only player to both captain and manage teams that won a World Cup (1974 and 1990, respectively).

6 Three words: hand of God.

7 Played on Brazil's winning World Cup teams in 1998 and 2002.

ANSWERS

1 Bobby Charlton

2 Lev Yashin

3 Pelé

4 Zinedine Zidane

5 Franz Beckenbauer

6 Diego Maradona

7 Ronaldo Luiz Nazario da Lima

Q What year did boxing become an Olympic sport?

A 688 BC. Boxing was part of the ancient Olympic Games and has been part of the modern Olympics since 1904. Women boxers competed for the first time at the 2012 Olympics in London.

⋙⋙⋙ **Four Unforgettable Boxing Matches** ⋘⋘⋘

1 Joe Louis vs. Max Schmeling (1938). American Joe Louis lost to Germany's Max Schmeling in 1936. Two years later, with Adolf Hitler leading Germany into World War II, Louis and Schmeling had a rematch. Louis managed a first-round knockout.

2 Sonny Liston vs. Cassius Clay (1964). Sonny Liston was the overwhelming favorite to beat Cassius Clay (aka Muhammad Ali) when they met for their first fight, in Miami. Liston conceded the match in the sixth round, claiming a hurt shoulder. This is the fight during which Clay pranced around the ring shouting, "I'm the greatest!"

3 George Foreman vs. Muhammad Ali (1974). This is the famous "Rumble in the Jungle" in Zaire, when the aging Muhammad Ali fought to regain his title against heavyweight champion George Foreman. Ali won it in the eighth round, with the fight announcer famously saying of Ali, "Oh my God! He's won it back at 32!"

4 Mike Tyson vs. Evander Holyfield (1997). Yeah, it's the heavyweight title fight during which Tyson bit off a section of Holyfield's ear. Enough said, really.

Q Why is the square boxing platform called a "ring"?

A Ancient Greek and Roman rules specified that combatants meet in a circular ring. They have been known as "rings" ever since.

Q How long have boxing gloves been required in professional boxing matches?

A Since 1892. Boxing was mostly fought with bare fists until the early nineteenth century. Gloves are intended to protect both your own hands and your opponent's face.

Q What sport does the WCBO govern?

A The World Chess Boxing Organization governs the amateur sport of chess boxing. That's right, boxing meets chess for eleven rounds in the ring! Competitors alternate between four-minute rounds of speed chess and three-minute rounds of honest-to-goodness boxing. The first chess boxer to earn checkmate or a knockout wins.

Q What sport does the MLE govern?

A Competitive eating. Major League Eating is a subsidiary of the International Federation of Competitive Eating, Inc. It doesn't matter what food is on offer, the goal of competitive eating contests is always the same: Eat as much as possible, as fast as possible. Arguably the most famous event is the annual Nathan's International Hot Dog Eating Contest, at which the goal is to eat the most hot dogs (yes, with bun) in 10 minutes. The current record of sixty-nine hot dogs is held by multi-award-winning eater Joey Chestnut.

Competitive Eating
⫸⫸⫸⫸ **Records from Major League Eating** ⫷⫷⫷⫷

- Butter: 7 sticks in 5 minutes by Don Lerman

- Chicken nuggets: 80 pieces in 5 minutes by Sonya Thomas

- Cupcakes: 42 in 8 minutes by Tim Janus

- Doughnuts: 49 glazed in 8 minutes by Eric Booker

- Eggs: 65 hardboiled in 6 minutes, 40 seconds by Sonya Thomas

- Haggis: 3 lb. in 8 minutes by Eric Livingston

- Jalapenos: 118 poppers in 10 minutes by Joey Chestnut

- Oysters: 46 dozen in 10 minutes by Sonya Thomas

- Sushi: 142 nigiri pieces in 6 minutes by Tim Janus

Q What sport does the WAF govern?

A Arm wrestling. The World Armwrestling Federation oversees this incredibly popular sport. Don't laugh—it's likely that arm wrestling will be included in a future Olympics. (Raise your hand if you paid to see the 1987 film *Over the Top* starring Sylvester Stallone as a truck driver turned arm wrestler. Nobody? Anybody? Fair enough. It was a terrible movie.)

Q What sport does the NTPA govern?

A Tractor pulling. The National Tractor Pullers Association is the leading organizing body in the United States and organizes annual Grand National Tractor Pull competitions. The idea is simple: Pull a sled loaded with weights over a 90-meter straight track, with the winner being whichever tractor can pull the heaviest load the farthest.

Q What biannual competition features the lady tickler, trash stash, crumb catcher, soul patch, handlebar, and tea strainer?

A The World Beard and Moustache Championship. Competitors are judged in seventeen different categories from "natural mustache" (mustache may be styled but without aids) and Dali mustache, to Fu Manchu and Full Beard Freestyle.

Q What international sporting event has featured winning performances by AC/DC, Van Halen, and Rage Against the Machine?

A The Air Guitar World Championships. Laugh all you want, air guitar is an ultra-competitive sport with its own world championships, held annually in Finland since 1996. Points are awarded for realism, stage presence, and "airness"—a subjective category similar to "presentation" in figure skating, i.e., the amount of kick-ass "airitude" the competitor exudes. In 2011, the gold medal was awarded for the first time to a woman (yes, boys, women play air guitar too).

Q What's the world record for longest time aloft of a successfully caught boomerang?

A Three minutes and 49 seconds. Wow. That's a long time aloft for anything without an engine.

Q What two oddball sporting events are held annually in the small Welsh village of Llanwrtyd Wells?

A The World Bog Snorkeling Championship and the Man Vs. Horse Marathon. In bog snorkeling, competitors wear flippers, mask, and snorkel, and swim as fast as possible through a peat-bog trench 60 yards long, 4 feet wide, and 5 feet deep. Standard swimming strokes are not allowed; competitors instead pull themselves along the bottom of the bog or use the doggy paddle. The man-versus-horse marathon is run over 22 miles (just shy of an official marathon) and pits around three hundred cross-country runners against forty to fifty riders on horseback. The original idea (fermented in a pub, of course) was to test the assumption that horses are faster than humans over long distances. The first race was run in 1980, and the horse won. It wasn't until 2004 that a human finally beat the horse.

Q What sport features googlies, grubbers, and jaffas?

A Cricket. All three are terms describing how balls are bowled or pitched: A googly is bowled with a deceptive spin, a grubber barely bounces on the ground, and a jaffa is a ball that is perfectly bowled and nearly impossible to strike.

Q What are the only ten teams allowed to play a sanctioned match of Test cricket?

A England, Australia, New Zealand, South Africa, Zimbabwe, West Indies, India, Pakistan, Bangladesh, and Sri Lanka. These are the only teams officially recognized by the International Cricket Council (ICC). Test teams play four-inning matches that can last up to five days.

Q Who invented the American sport of baseball?

A Unknown. And it's a trick question. Most people would say Abner Doubleday invented baseball in Cooperstown, New York, in 1839. But that's a myth. Baseball is likely a derivative of the British and Irish game called rounders. There is no single inventor of the modern American game.

Q What team won the first recorded game of baseball?

A The New York Nine. They beat the New York Knickerbockers 23 to 1 in 1846. By 1857, sixteen New York-area clubs were playing baseball under the auspices of the National Association of Base Ball Players (NABBP), the sport's very first governing body.

Q What year was the first World Series played?

A 1903. The Boston Americans (American League) beat the Pittsburgh Pirates (National League) in a best-of-nine game series. Five years later, the Boston Americans rebranded themselves the Boston Red Sox.

Did you know?

Early forms of baseball allowed throwing the ball at a runner for an out and pitching underhanded. Balls caught on one bounce were considered outs.

Q What major league baseball team has famously not won a World Series since 1908?

A The Chicago Cubs. And what's the reason for the drought? If you believe the myth, it's due to a curse put on the team by the owner of the Billy Goat Tavern, Billy Sianis. At the 1945 World Series, between the Detroit Tigers and Chicago Cubs, Sianis was asked to leave the game because the aroma of his pet goat was offensive to nearby fans. Naturally, Sianis hexed the Cubs. And the team has not won a World Series or a National League pennant since. Believe it or not, in a futile attempt to break the curse, the nephew of Billy Sianis has been invited—and appeared more than once!—accompanied by a goat at Wrigley Field, home of the Chicago Cubs. No luck breaking the hex, but a fantastic photo op for a man and his goat.

Q Who invented the high five?

A Most sources credit Glenn Burke of the Los Angeles Dodgers. During the final game of the 1977 regular season, Dodger player Dusty Baker hit a home run and was greeted in the dugout with an up-high fist slap by teammate Glenn Burke. The rest is history.

Q What's the most popular sport in the United States?

A Professional football, if you judge it by television-viewing statistics.

Q When was the first Super Bowl played?

A 1967. The Green Bay Packers beat the Kansas City Chiefs, 35–10.

Q When was the modern game of football invented?

A It's murky, but you can reasonably argue that modern
American football was invented in 1880. That's the year
that the rules proposed by Walter Camp, an enthusiast and
early pioneer of the game, were ratified by a core group of
East Coast colleges. It was Camp who suggested teams of
eleven players and who developed the concepts of a "line of
scrimmage," and snapping balls by hand from a center to
a quarterback. Camp later championed a requirement to
advance the ball a minimum of five yards in three downs.

Did you know?

The early years of American football were tumultuous
due to concerns about player safety. The University
of California at Berkeley's rugby team, for example,
was disbanded in 1886 in favor of the newly popular
sport of football, brought back from 1906 to 1914
when football was deemed too violent, and replaced
by football a second time, in 1914.

Q Who is credited with instituting the forward-pass rule in
football?

A President Theodore Roosevelt. He demanded a change to
football's rules in 1905, after eighteen players were killed and
159 injured that year. The forward pass was intended to open
up the game and to minimize the chaotic dog piles associated
with lateral passes. The rule was adopted in 1906.

Q What's the average amount of play time in a National Football League (NFL) game?

A Eleven minutes. That's eleven minutes of actual play achieved over four 15-minute quarters.

Q What's the only current NFL team playing in its original city, under its original name?

A The Chicago Bears. They've been the Chicago Bears since 1921.

Q Who are the Buffalo Bills named for?

A Showman, soldier, and bison hunter Buffalo Bill Cody. The name comes from a 1947 fan contest to rename the team originally known as the Buffalo Bisons.

Q What was the original name of the Oakland Raiders?

A The Oakland Señors. It was the winning entry in a 1959 contest sponsored by the *Oakland Tribune* to name the new franchise. The name was a heartfelt tribute to the early settlers of California, but fans were not impressed. Nine days after rolling out the new name, the owners opted for the third-place entry, Raiders.

Q What are the San Diego Chargers named after?

A The bugle chant, "Charge!" The team's original owner, Barron Hilton, heir to the Hilton Hotels fortune, liked the name because it reminded him of the yells of "charge" he had heard at other major sporting events.

Q Who's the only athlete to have played in both a Super Bowl and a World Series?

A Deion Sanders. In 1989, he played in the Super Bowl for the Atlanta Falcons and in the World Series for the New York Yankees. He's also the only person to have scored a touchdown and hit a major league homerun in the same week.

Q Who invented the Nerf football?

A Fred Cox. He was a kicker for the Minnesota Vikings and came up with the idea of a soft foam football while playing in the NFL. He still earns royalties on every Nerf football sold.

Q What was the NFL minimum pay for a rookie football player in 2014?

A More than $420,000.

Q What percent of professional football players are bankrupt or in severe financial troubles after retiring from the NFL?

A Seventy eight percent. That's after just *two years* of retirement.

⟫⟫⟫⟫⟫ **The Best Fictional Sports, Ever!** ⟪⟪⟪⟪⟪

- BASEketball. This sport comes from the 1998 film of the same name, starring *South Park* creators Matt Stone and Trey Parker (as well as Ernest Borgnine— extra points for casting!). The idea is simple, in a totally stupid way: Start with baseball, but instead of hitting a ball with a stick, players sink basketball shots in order to move around the bases.

- Brockian Ultra-Cricket. Douglas Adams's book *The Hitchhiker's Guide to the Galaxy* includes the marvelously curious sport of Brockian Ultra-Cricket. Players should hit each other as hard as possible with cricket bats, basecube bats, tennis guns, skis, or anything that delivers a hearty, swinging smack. When you score a hit on an opposing player, run far away and apologize from a safe distance.

- Death Race. The 1975 film *Death Race 2000* stars Sly Stallone and David Carradine. The eponymous Death Race involves driving whacked-out cars across the U.S., earning points by smashing into spectators (extra points for old people and babies).

- Gumball Rally. This classic 1976 film features a coast-to-coast rally race by drivers who only need to have the word "gumball" whispered in their ear to hit the road in souped-up street cars. It's an old-school car race, full of gentle shenanigans.

- Jugging. What, you've never heard of the 1989 movie *Blood of Heroes*? Tsk tsk. It's the one with Rutger Hauer *and* Vincent D'Onofrio. The object of jugging is to place a dog skull (called the "jug") on the opposing team's stake in the ground. Only one player from each team can touch the skull; he's called the "qwik." Also on the field is a player called "the chain" (armed with a chain weapon) and three "enforcers" (each brandishing swords and pikes). The chain and enforcers are there

- Quidditch. The quintessential Harry Potter sport is an airborne combination of soccer, basketball, and hockey. Goals are scored by chucking a ball called the quaffle through one of the opponent's three goals (worth 10 points). A quidditch match can end on a moment's notice if either team captures the golden snitch, a walnut-sized winged ball that makes unpredictable appearances during the match.

- Rollerball. The idea of this awesome 1975 movie is that, in the future, corporations have replaced all governments and use the sport of rollerball to control the masses. Rollerball itself is played by teams on roller skates and motorcycles (yes!) attempting to throw a magnetized steel ball through a metal hoop. Strategy tip? Don't put your head in front of the cannon that fires the steel ball at the start of each possession.

- Triad. This one comes from the television series *Battlestar Galactica* (the original version). It's a contact sport with elements of football and basketball, played on a triangular court by two coed teams of two players. It's all the rage in the Twelve Colonies.

- Tron. It's the pentathlon of the future. Get sucked into a computer and don your glow-in-the-dark unitard in preparation for five different athletic competitions courtesy of the 1982 film *Tron*.

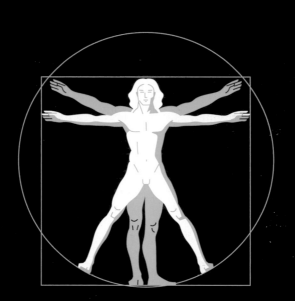

BEING HUMAN

CHAPTER 4

Being Human

Q What do approximately one in eighteen men have?

A A third nipple. Third nipples run the gamut from small, dark patches of hair easily mistaken for moles to miniature nipples capable of bearing milk. In the seventeenth century, women with third nipples were accused of suckling the Devil and, ipso facto, were "exposed" as witches.

Q What do Tilda Swinton, Carrie Underwood, Lily Allen, and Mark Wahlberg have in common?

A They all have third nipples. Mark Wahlberg's third nipple was airbrushed out in his famous Calvin Klein underwear ads.

 **Did you know?**

People with third nipples sometimes suffer from atelophobia, the fear of being imperfect.

Q Why do men have nipples in the first place?

A Not to be a smart ass, but men have nipples because women
   have nipples. They are a shared genetic trait, much like eyes
   and ears and noses. While it's not clear if nipples have always
   been used to deliver milk to infants, in females, nipples are a
   linchpin of reproductive success. In males, however, they are
   inconsequential appendages. And body parts that do no harm
   tend to stick around, whether they're pelvis bones in whales or
   nipples in men.

Q What is odontophobia?

A The fear of teeth, especially animal teeth.

Q What is acarophobia?

A The fear of skin infestations with worms, mites, or small
   crawling animals.

Q What is ailurophobia?

A The persistent and irrational fear of cats.

Q What is alektorophobia?

A The fear of chickens.

Q What is barophobia?

A The irrational fear of gravity (as in, being crushed by).

Q What is pogonophobia?

A The fear of beards and facial hair.

Did you know?

In ancient times beards were a sign of strength and wisdom, and they were only cut or sheared off as a punishment or in mourning.

Q How fast does a man's beard grow?

A On average, the whiskers in a man's beard grow nearly six inches per year. It's the same for most hair on the human body, all of which is dead and grows about half an inch per month, or six inches per year. Men's beards grow bushier in summer, due to seasonal variations in the amount of the steroid dihydrotestosterone in their bodies.

Q What are the only places on the human body where hair does not grow?

A Soles of the feet, palms of the hands, lips, and eyelids (not counting eyelashes).

Q How long can fingernails grow?

A The *Guinness Book of World Records* credits India's Shridhar Chillal with having the longest fingernails ever recorded. Chillal did not cut his fingernails between 1952 and 2000, and his longest nail was 4.25 feet. The women's record for longest fingernails belongs to Lee Redmond. The nail on her right thumb was measured at 2 feet, 11 inches. It took her thirty years to grow that nail.

Q Which grows faster, fingernails or toenails?

A Fingernails. They grow four times faster than your toenails, at roughly the same rate at which continental drift occurs, approximately a tenth of an inch per month.

Q Do your fingernails all grow at the same rate?

A No. The nail on your index finger grows faster than the nail on your pinky finger.

Q What does it mean if your index finger is shorter than your ring finger?

A If you're a man, it means you're one-third more likely to be diagnosed with prostate cancer. Scientists think that men with longer index fingers have lower levels of testosterone, which offers some protection against prostate cancer. Interestingly, different studies have found that men with longer index fingers earn more money and are more aggressive (i.e., less emotionally attuned).

Q Why is the sound of nails scratching a chalkboard so horrible?

A This is a real phenomenon. Recent studies suggest that the human ear canal amplifies sounds in the 2,000 and 4,000 hertz range—which is precisely where the nails-on-chalkboard screech registers. The amplification can be perceived as painful.

Q What does it mean if you have a crease in your earlobes?

A It means you are at risk to suffer from coronary artery disease. Additionally, for men, having an earlobe crease means you're significantly more likely to suffer a heart attack.

Q How fast does your heart pump blood?

A Blood circulates through the human body on average every twenty-three seconds, and the adult human heart pumps about four thousand gallons of blood each day.

Q Over the course of your life, how many times will your heart beat?

A The average human heart beats 3 billion times over its lifetime.

Did you know?

Your heartbeat mimics the music you listen to and can trigger physiological changes that increase or decrease your blood pressure.

So yes, there is a physiological difference between listening to Fugazi versus Bob Marley.

TRUE OR FALSE? Your left lung is slightly smaller than your right lung.

TRUE.

It's to allow room for your heart.

TRUE OR FALSE? It's impossible to lick your own elbow.

FALSE.

Trust us, the answer is *false*.

TRUE OR FALSE? The longest recorded bout of hiccups lasted for sixty-eight years.

TRUE.

Charles Osborne, a hog farmer from Iowa, began hiccupping in 1922 and did not stop until 1990 at age 97, a year before his death. He hiccupped between twenty and forty times per minute.

TRUE OR FALSE? The longest time somebody has kept his eyes open without blinking is twenty-four minutes.

TRUE.

TRUE OR FALSE? The longest time somebody has kept one eye open without blinking is eight minutes and twenty-six seconds.

TRUE.

TRUE OR FALSE? Sneezing with your eyes open can cause your eyeballs to pop out from your head.

FALSE.

It's a myth. Rest assured that if your eyes *were* going to pop out of your head, your eyelids would not be strong enough to prevent it from happening. So go ahead, sneeze with your eyes open.

TRUE OR FALSE? Bright light and sunshine can make you sneeze.

TRUE.

"Sternutators" are things that can make you sneeze, and both sunlight and bright light are included on the list.

TRUE OR FALSE? A sneeze can release particles from your nose at speeds that can break the sound barrier.

FALSE.

Sneezes aren't nearly that fast. The television show *Mythbusters* has measured sneezes up to 39 miles per hour. The fastest sneezes measured in a lab clock in at 102 miles per hour.

TRUE OR FALSE? The heaviest weight lifted by a human tongue is more than fifty pounds.

FALSE.

According to Guinness World Records, the heaviest weight lifted by a human tongue is just over twenty-seven pounds, a record set by Thomas Blackthorne in 2008.

TRUE OR FALSE? Right-handed people live, on average, nine years longer than left-handed people.

TRUE.

TRUE OR FALSE? Approximately 10 percent of both modern homo sapien and now extinct Neanderthal populations show a preference for their left hand.

TRUE.

TRUE OR FALSE? The word "left" is derived from words that mean weak and defective.

TRUE.

The word "left" comes from the Anglo-Saxon word "lyft," which means "weak" or "not working." The Oxford English Dictionary gives synonyms of "left-handed" that include defective, awkward, illegitimate, and characterized by underhanded dealings. In many Islamic countries it is forbidden to eat with the left hand, which is considered unclean because it is used for cleaning the body after defecation.

Did you know?

August 13 is International Left-Hander's Day.

TRUE OR FALSE? Redheads are more likely than other people to be left-handed.

TRUE.

TRUE OR FALSE? About 10 percent of people are natural redheads.

FALSE.

Only about 2 percent of people are natural redheads. Red hair is a recessive trait, which means you must inherit one red hair gene from each parent.

TRUE OR FALSE? Redheads don't usually go gray.

TRUE.

It's because red hair retains its natural pigment longer than other shades of hair.

TRUE OR FALSE? Ireland has more redheads than any other country.

FALSE.

Scotland has the highest proportion of redheads in the world, at 13 percent. Ireland comes in second at 10 percent. Redheads may have pale skin, but this allows them to generate their own vitamin D and to thrive in low-light environments!

Did you know?

Common surnames in the British Isles include Flanary ("red eyebrow"), Reid ("red-haired"), and Flynn ("reddish complexion").

TRUE OR FALSE? Red hair and blue eyes is the rarest combination in the world.

TRUE.

The majority of natural redheads have brown eyes.

➤ **DO YOU EVER FEEL LIKE A BANANA? OR MAYBE A CHICKEN? MATCH THE PERCENTAGE OF DNA THAT HUMANS SHARE WITH THE FOLLOWING:**

1	Bonobo monkeys	A	97.5 percent
2	Orangutans	B	44 percent
3	Lettuce	C	18 percent
4	Mice	D	96.9 percent
5	Honey bees	E	11 percent
6	Baker's yeast	F	50 percent
7	Chickens	G	98.2 percent
8	Bananas	H	65 percent

ANSWERS

1G, 2D, 3E, 4A, 5B, 6C, 7H, 8F

TRUE OR FALSE? Humans sweat up to a pint of fluid at night.

TRUE.

And unevaporated sweat in your bedsheets and mattress are a ripe breeding ground for parasites, mold, and mildew.

TRUE OR FALSE? Humans can survive longer without food than they can without sleep.

TRUE.

The longest any person has gone without sleep (verified) not using stimulants or other drugs is 264 hours, or about eleven days. The longest a person has gone without food or water (total starvation) is seventy-three days.

TRUE OR FALSE? Sleeping with an electric blanket can interrupt your sleep patterns and make it difficult to get a good night's sleep.

TRUE.

TRUE OR FALSE? The optimal sleep temperature for humans is 68 degrees.

HALF TRUE.

Sleep scientists generally agree that restful nights of sleep are most common between 54 and 75 degrees Fahrenheit. The general rule of thumb is to sleep in a slightly cool room, because this matches what happens inside your own body as your internal temperature drops during the night.

TRUE OR FALSE? Up until the late nineteenth century, most people slept in two shifts separated by a long period of wakefulness.

TRUE.

Before electricity was commonplace, people slept an average of nine hours divided into two segments: four to five hours of sleep, an hour of wakefulness, and four to five hours of more sleep. The hour of wakefulness was a time for smoking, having sex, visiting neighbors, or writing poetry. Today, in the post-industrial era, we average no more than seven hours of sleep per night—one full hour less than what's considered normal and necessary for good health.

TRUE OR FALSE? You cannot snore and dream at the same time.

FALSE.

You can—and often do—manage both at the same time, considering that you dream for more than two full hours each night.

TRUE OR FALSE? Most dreams last for only a few seconds.

FALSE.

We dream at least four to six times a night, with the longest dreams in the morning lasting a full thirty to forty-five minutes.

TRUE OR FALSE? Women and men need about the same amount of sleep per night.

FALSE.

Women need an hour's extra sleep compared to men, though they often do not get it. Not getting the extra hour of sleep is believed to be one reason women are more susceptible to depression than men.

TRUE OR FALSE? Earwax is not wax.

TRUE.

Ear wax (officially called cerumen) is a waxy mix of oil, sweat, and dead skin cells that forms inside the ear and slowly migrates to the outer ear, where it dries and flakes away.

TRUE OR FALSE? Itchiness is contagious.

TRUE.

Itchiness is contagious in humans. Merely watching a person scratch makes the brain think it is experiencing an itch, even when it is not.

TRUE OR FALSE? You are more susceptible to contagious itches if you are neurotic, anxious, or depressed.

TRUE.

And so unfair!

TRUE OR FALSE? You shed about forty thousand skin cells per minute.

TRUE.

Most of those forty thousand dead skin cells are brushed away as flakes. And it goes without saying that each day you inhale thousands of your own dead skin flakes. While shedding forty thousand flakes a minute sounds like a large amount, keep in mind that skin on the average adult measures 20 square feet and accounts for 12 percent of body weight.

TRUE OR FALSE? The average bed is home to 10 million dust mites.

TRUE.

TRUE OR FALSE? Your skin houses billions of individual bacteria.

TRUE.

And that's billion with a "b." The good news? Inhaling all that bacteria means you're less likely to develop allergies and asthma. Studies show you're more susceptible to allergies if you grow up in an extremely clean environment lacking bacterial variety.

TRUE OR FALSE? Your belly button is home to more than sixty strains of bacteria.

TRUE.

The average person has sixty-seven different strains of bacteria living in his belly button. In a recent sample of 66 people, researchers found more than 2,368 different species of bacteria living in the belly button. Belly button bacteria are amazingly diverse. Fewer than ten bacterial species occurred in more than half of all people screened. Two samples in the belly button study contained a single-cell organism called arachea, which had never before been found on human skin.

TRUE OR FALSE? The most common bacterium in your belly button is the same species that make your feet smell.

TRUE.

The most common bacteria in the belly button include *Staphylococci*, which protect skin from unhealthy germs, and *Bacillus*, an anti-fungal bacterium that is also responsible for making your feet stinky.

TRUE OR FALSE? Nearly every person alive is home to thousands of tiny parasitic mites.

TRUE.

The mites live in your hair follicles (eyelashes, eyebrows, etc.), have eight legs, and walk around on your skin at night . . . before returning to your hair follicles at dawn.

TRUE OR FALSE? Hair mites are not dangerous.

MOSTLY TRUE.

Hair mites generally go unnoticed and cause no harm except when you're sick or under stress—times when your mite population can increase dramatically and cause swollen eyelids, itchy skin, and acne.

TRUE OR FALSE? Some tumors inside your body can grow hair and teeth.

TRUE.

The teratoma tumor is found in humans and has the ability to grow hair, teeth, and even bone. In rare cases these tumors can grow eyes, hands, and feet too!

TRUE OR FALSE? Tapeworms inside humans have been measured up to 20 feet long.

TRUE.

The longest tapeworm in humans is the *D. latum*, which averages 20 feet in length. What's worse? Adult tapeworms can lay more than a million eggs per day in their human hosts. What's even worse? The larvae of tapeworms often grow inside the human body hidden in large sack-like cysts. These cysts can be dislodged from whatever tissue they are anchored to and end up in people's brains, causing a disease known as neurocysticercosis.

TRUE OR FALSE? The largest hairball removed from a human weighed five pounds.

FALSE.

It actually weighed ten pounds! Not only that, it also measured 15 inches in diameter. It was a massive tangle of curly black hair removed by doctors after the patient complained of abdominal pains and frequent vomiting. Not surprisingly, the patient also suffered from a condition called trichophagia—or eating one's own hair.

TRUE OR FALSE? If you suffer from Uner Tan syndrome, it means you're a human quadruped.

TRUE.

Uner Tan syndrome causes people to walk on all fours and speak in a primitive style of Ur speech. What's worse? The genetic disorder Hutchinson-Gilford Progeria, which causes accelerated aging. Children afflicted with the rare disease typically die at 13 years of age from age-related conditions such as stroke and heart attacks.

TRUE OR FALSE? The average adult toenail is home to forty-three species of fungi.

TRUE.

Fungi thrive on humans by feeding on keratin, a protein found in skin, hair, and nails.

TRUE OR FALSE? If you suffer from autonomous sensory meridian response (ASMR) it means you find the sounds of whispering deeply satisfying.

TRUE.

ASMR is not yet an approved medical diagnosis. Yet thousands of people claim the sounds of breathy whispers, gentle taps, and the rustling of paper relieve stress and help with insomnia. What, you've never searched YouTube for ASMR videos?! Off you go, and have fun. The videos range from bizarre to creepy to borderline perverted.

TRUE OR FALSE? If you suffer from Dunning–Kruger bias, you think other people are less competent than you.

TRUE.

If you're unskilled or not very smart, you tend to overestimate your own skills and underestimate the skills of others. This cognitive bias explains a lot about the United States.

TRUE OR FALSE? If you sufferer from Trimethylaminuria, you literally stink like rotten fish.

TRUE.

Also known as Fish Odor Syndrome, Trimethylaminuria is caused by a build-up of a pungent-smelling chemical in your body that is normally metabolized and eliminated in your urine and sweat. The good news? Trimethylaminuria is a genetic disorder, and both of your parents need to possess mutated versions of the same gene. The less good news? If one of your parents has the mutation, you're likely to experience temporary episodes of strong body odor throughout your life—the kind of body odor that standard antiperspirants and deodorants won't come close to masking.

TRUE OR FALSE? The word "fart" is one of the oldest words in the English language.

TRUE.

TRUE OR FALSE? Benjamin Franklin wrote an essay about farts and flatulence called "Fart Proudly."

TRUE.

Franklin wrote the infamous essay while he was living in France as the United States Ambassador.

TRUE OR FALSE? Men and women fart about the same amount each day.

TRUE.

Despite rumors to the contrary, men and women fart equally—about half a liter of gas per day.

TRUE OR FALSE? People who swallow a lot of air fart more than people who don't.

TRUE.

The corollary is also true. Chew with your mouth closed and you will fart less.

TRUE OR FALSE? All farts smell the same.

FALSE.

Farts smell because of the sulfurous gases they contain. Not all farts are created equal: Meat, eggs, broccoli, and cauliflower cause the smelliest farts. Beans contain little sulfur but a lot of gas-producing sugars. Which means eating beans generates a large amount of not-so-smelly gas. Other high-sugar foods that produce not-so-smelly farts include corn, bell peppers, cabbage, and raisins.

TRUE OR FALSE? Holding in your farts makes them smell worse.

FALSE.

Only 1 percent of fart gases are pungent. The other 99 percent are odorless. And the sulfurous 1 percent is not affected by how long you hold the gas inside your bowels.

TRUE OR FALSE? Farts travel faster than the speed of sound when leaving your body.

FALSE.

C'mon, faster than the speed of sound? In reality, farts leave the body at approximately 10 feet per second, or roughly 7 miles per hour.

TRUE OR FALSE? Farts are highly flammable.

TRUE.

> Just ask any college freshman. Farts contain methane and hydrogen, two highly flammable gasses, and tend to burn with a blue or yellow flame.

 **Did you know?**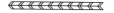

> Defecaloesiophobia is the fear of painful bowel movements.

Q What is human excrement made of?

A Approximately 75 percent water, 10 percent dead bacteria, and 10 percent indigestible fiber. The remaining 5 percent is a mix of fats, salts, live bacteria, and mucus from the lining of the intestines.

Q Why is human poop brown?

A The brown color comes from bilirubin, a pigment produced from the degradation of hemoglobin and red blood cells. Without iron in your diet, your poop would not be brown. Too much iron in your diet can turn your poop green.

Q Why does human poop float?

A It doesn't always float. Poop only floats when it has a high concentration of undissolved gases, usually produced by bacteria in the digestive system.

Q Is it safe to eat human poop?

A No. (Um, did anybody actually say "yes"?) Poop generally contains high levels of bacteria. Many parasites and diseases, including cholera and typhus, are spread by fecal contamination. Human poop is also responsible for the decline of numerous corals in the Caribbean ocean.

Q When is World Toilet Day?

A November 19, according to the United Nations.

Q What percentage of the world's population lacks access to a flushing toilet?

A More than 40 percent. What's worse? Every day more than 15 percent of the world's population defecates outside in the open air, and not by choice.

Q Which is healthier, pooping standing up or sitting down?

A Standing up. You suffer fewer hemorrhoids and fewer colonic obstructions by pooping standing up. The taller the toilet, the worse it is.

Q Which is healthier, wiping sitting down or standing up?

A There is no health difference.

Q Who was named the third best-known American in 1978?

A The fictional Mr. Whipple ("Please don't squeeze the Charmin!"). He was named the third best-known American just behind former President Nixon and evangelist Billy Graham.

➤ CONTAGIOUS YAWNING IN PEOPLE IS LESS LIKELY TO HAPPEN IN WHICH SEASON?

A Spring

B Summer

C Winter

D Fall

ANSWER

B. A critical function of yawning is to cool down the brain. Warmer ambient air temperatures mean the usefulness of a yawn is diminished. So contagious yawning is least likely in summer.

➤ THE SMELL OF WOMEN'S TEARS IS MORE LIKELY TO MAKE MEN FEEL WHAT?

A Less sexually aroused

B More sexually aroused

C Less sympathetic to others

D More sympathetic to others

ANSWER

A. Human tears have a chemosignaling function. For reasons not fully understood, the smell of women's tears makes men feel less sexually aroused and reduces levels of testosterone.

A   25 minutes

B   90 minutes

C   45 minutes

D   15 minutes

ANSWER

Trick question. It's both A and B. According to sleep scientists, naps of durations other than twenty-five or ninety minutes will make you feel more tired and groggy when you wake up.

➤ HAPPY PEOPLE ARE LESS LIKELY TO WHAT?

A   Get a tattoo

B   Smoke cigarettes

C   Catch a cold

D   Snore at night

ANSWER

C. Studies have shown that people who self-report as happy are less likely to become ill when exposed to either a rhinovirus or influenza virus. The good news for unhappy people? Being depressed or feeling similar negative emotions does not make you more likely to catch a cold.

➤ **COMPARED TO STRAIGHT HAIR, WHAT IS CURLY HAIR LESS LIKELY TO DO?**

A Fall out

B Become oily

C Get tangled

D Turn prematurely gray

ANSWER

C. Somewhat counterintuitively, curly hair has fewer tangles than straight hair. In one study, people with straight hair had an average of 5.3 tangles compared to only 2.9 tangles for people with curly hair.

➤ **COMPARED TO SHORTER PEOPLE, TALLER PEOPLE ARE MORE LIKELY TO WHAT?**

A Have higher IQs

B Be bitten by bugs

C Earn more money

D Develop blood clots

E All of the above

ANSWER

E. Tall people are smarter, exhale greater quantities of bug-attracting carbon dioxide, earn more money on average, and are more at risk to develop blood clots in the legs. Don't get too depressed if you're short: You will live longer than your taller, smarter, and wealthier tall peers.

A   They have a heightened ability to perceive colors

B   They have a higher tolerance for alcohol

C   They are more likely to have cataracts

D   They have lower IQs

ANSWER

B. On the plus side, people with blue eyes can drink more before exhibiting signs of drunkenness. On the downside, if you have blue eyes you're also more likely to be an alcoholic compared to people with brown eyes.

➤ IF THE DNA IN EVERY CELL OF YOUR BODY WAS UNCOILED, HOW FAR WOULD IT STRETCH?

A   100,000 miles

B   1 million miles

C   1 billion miles

D   10 billion miles

ANSWER

D. And that's a lot of DNA.

HISTORY

POLITICS

• CHAPTER 5 •

History & Politics

TRUE OR FALSE? History began in the fifth century BC.

TRUE.

> History is *written* history. Before that everything is considered "prehistoric" by scholars. Hellenic Greeks in the fifth century BC made written records of political events and put them into a wider social context. So it's not wrong to say Hellenic Greeks invented history.

TRUE OR FALSE? Written language was invented independently by the Sumerians, Egyptians, Chinese, and Maya.

TRUE.

TRUE OR FALSE? All languages on Earth are derived from a single ancient language.

TRUE, MOST LIKELY.

> Mounting evidence suggests that all human languages—from Chinese to Icelandic to Sanskrit to English—come from a single "mother tongue" spoken in sub-Saharan Africa more than 100,000 years ago.

TRUE OR FALSE? The world's first city was in Iraq.

TRUE.

Most scholars consider Uruk, south of Baghdad in modern Iraq, as the world's first city. It was settled around 4500 BC. Extra points if you know that its most famous king was Gilgamesh.

Did you know?

Uruk may be the oldest city on Earth, but the Egyptian city of Faiyum is the oldest continuously inhabited city. It's been going strong since about 4000 BC.

TRUE OR FALSE? The reign of the world's first recorded king, Alulim, lasted for 28,800 years.

TRUE, BUT WITH A CAVEAT.

Records from the ancient Akkadian empire list Alulim as the first recorded king, taking the throne shortly after said throne descended from the heavens. It's not clear if Alulim is a real person or mythical. According to the Akkadians, his rule lasted for a really, really, really long time—nearly twenty-nine thousand years.

TRUE OR FALSE? Cleopatra lived nearer in time to the moon landing than to the building of the Great Pyramid of Giza.

TRUE.

Cleopatra was born in 69 BC. The Great Pyramid of Giza was built around 2540 BC. The moon landing happened in 1969. You do the math.

TRUE OR FALSE? After ruling for thirty years, some Egyptian pharaohs were required to run around a special track four times in order to prove their physical fitness to rule.

TRUE.

And what a great way to deal with term limits.

TRUE OR FALSE? The first female king in recorded history is also considered one of the most successful.

TRUE.

Hatshepsut, who ruled Egypt for more than twenty years in the fifteenth century BC, is considered one of Egypt's most capable pharaohs.

TRUE OR FALSE? The great pyramids of Egypt were built by slaves.

FALSE.

Most workers were paid for the back-breaking work of building the pyramids.

TRUE OR FALSE? The workers who built the Egyptian pyramids were paid in beer.

TRUE.

Workers received a daily beer ration of four to five liters. No beer, no pyramids.

TRUE OR FALSE? The Great Pyramid of Giza was the world's tallest structure for more than 3,800 years.

TRUE.

Its 2.3 million stone blocks originally rose to a height of 481 feet. Not only was it the tallest manmade monument on Earth for millennia, it is also the only ancient wonder of the world that still exists today.

TRUE OR FALSE? The Olympics are older than Homer's *Iliad* and *Odyssey*.

FALSE.

The first Olympics were held in 776 BC; most scholars say Homer lived and wrote circa 850 BC.

POP QUIZ

Kingly Nicknames

Q

Which of the following nicknames will you find in royal history books—and which are fakes?

1 The Dung Named

2 The Elbow-High

3 The Gouty

4 Hairy Breeches

5 The Hunchback

6 The Memorable

7 Special Unique

8 Minus-a-Quarter

9 Moneybags

10 The Be-Shitten

ANSWERS

1 Real. Constantine V earned his nickname after usurping the Byzantine throne in Constantinople (modern-day Istanbul). The losers called him Constantine the Dung-Named, insinuating that he took a poop in his baptismal font.

2   Real. Władysław I of Poland wasn't especially short. He was not clever enough to inspire a more interesting nickname than "elbow high," however.

3   Real. Bermudo II of León was not a great king. He lost many battles and famously suffered from gout. His subjects preferred to remember him for the gout.

4   Real. Ragnar Lodbrok (yes—him of History Channel's *Vikings* series) may have been a myth, nobody is sure. Mythical or not, his nickname is real. Romans didn't wear pants, so they insulted the "barbaric" Germanic tribes by suggesting they wore cloth or breeches around the legs.

5   Real. Pepin the Hunchback was the eldest son of Charlemagne.

6   Real. Denmark's Erik II was an unpopular and brutal king. Displaying a nice sense of irony, his subjects tagged him with the sobriquet "memorable."

7   Fake. There's never been a king known as Special Unique.

8   Real. Michael VII Dukas was an emperor of Byzantium. He levied unpopular taxes, let the army deteriorate, and allowed large parts of the Byzantine kingdom in Asia Minor to be conquered. He also allowed the currency to be devalued. For this crime he is known to eternity as Michael VII Minus-a-Quarter.

9   Real. Ivan I of Moscow was not a wealthy Wall Street
    executive flaunting his gold and jewels. Rather he used his
    wealth and connections to make Moscow itself wealthy and
    the heart of the nascent Russian empire.

10 Real. The moral of the story here is—don't cross the Irish.
    James II was the king of England, a Roman Catholic who
    bristled at the authority of England's Anglican Church. Long
    story short: James' nephew, William III of Orange, invaded
    England and forced James to flee. James attempted to
    recover his crown by landing an army in Ireland. Being
    on the losing side at the Battle of the Boyne, however,
    James fled Ireland for France, never to return. The Irish
    felt abandoned by James, blessing him with the nickname
    James the Shit or James the Be-Shitten.

Q   King Zog I ruled what country?

A   Albania. Zog was easier to pronounce than his given name,
    Ahmet Muhtar Bej Zogoll.

Q   What is the claim to fame of Swaziland's Sobhuza II?

A   He is the longest-ruling king ever, at least among rulers
    whose dates can be verified. After governing Swaziland for a
    remarkable eighty-two years and 254 days, Sobhuza II passed
    away quietly in 1984.

Q What's the shortest reign of a modern monarch?

A About twenty minutes. Louis-Antoine became king of France in 1830. He abdicated very shortly thereafter.

Q Who's the king of Vatican City?

A It's not a trick question—the pope is king. The Lateran Treaty of 1929 established Vatican City as an independent state with a monarch. Since then the pope has not only kept the keys to Heaven, he's also been the elected monarch of Vatican City (three cheers for absolute theocracies!).

Q What do Belgium, Denmark, Norway, Spain, Sweden, and the United Kingdom have in common?

A They are all functioning monarchies with kings, queens, princes, and princesses.

Q What do Mr. Christian Mowatt and Miss Zenouska Mowatt share in common, besides a last name?

A They are brother and sister and currently stand fiftieth and fifty-first in line to inherit the British throne. Who knew the royal queue was so long?

Q How did King Henry I of England die?

A He ate too many fish—too many lampreys, to be precise. His physician had apparently warned him of the dangers of eating too many lampreys, but hey, Henry I couldn't say no to a heaping plate of jawless sucker-fish.

Q How did Britain's George II die?

A On the toilet, of a heart attack. How royally incommodious.

Q What is George II's grandson, King George III, famously
  remembered for?

A Take your pick—for losing the American Revolutionary War
  and presiding over a vast decrease in the size and prestige of
  the British crown, and for being dotty. He was the "mad" King
  George of film fame, removed from the throne while living due
  to mental illness.

Q In which of Britain's thirteen American colonies was slavery
  outlawed?

A None. Slavery was legal, and common, in all thirteen American
  colonies.

Q The Bahamas, Barbados, Louisiana, Florida, and Nova
  Scotia—which was *not* ruled by the British in the 1770s?

A Louisiana. Score yourself an extra point for knowing that
  Louisiana was governed by Spain at the time. Give yourself an
  extra pat on the back for knowing that France gained control
  of Louisiana in 1800.

Q Everybody knows George Washington was the first American
  president. Who were the second, third, and fourth?

A John Adams, Thomas Jefferson, and James Madison. Couldn't
  name a single one? Don't feel too bad. A survey by the United
  States Mint in 2007 found that only 7 percent of Americans
  can name the first four presidents in order!

Q Who was the shortest U.S. president, at 5 feet, 4 inches?

A James Madison.

Q Which U.S. president weighed the least?

A Good ol' James Madison again, weighing in at less than 100 pounds.

Q Who was the heaviest U.S. president?

A William Howard Taft. During his time in office he weighed more than 300 pounds. He was so fat (shout it: how fat was he?) that he once got stuck in a White House bathtub. Literally.

Did you know?

Beyond his weight, Taft is remembered for being the first U.S. president to throw a pitch on the opening day of baseball season. Since then every president except Jimmy Carter has followed suit.

Q Who was the tallest U.S. president?

A Honest Abe Lincoln. He topped the charts at 6 feet, 4 inches.

Q George Washington or Ronald Reagan—who was taller?

A Washington had Reagan by an inch, 6 feet, 2 inches versus 6 feet, 1 inch.

Q Who is the only U.S. president to have killed somebody in a duel?

A Andrew "Badass" Jackson.

Q   Who is the only U.S. president to have taken a bullet in the arm during a bar fight?

A   Andrew "Badass" Jackson.

Q   Which U.S. president had a pet parrot who could swear— and who swore mightily at the funeral of the very same U.S. president, to the dismay of pretty much everybody in attendance?

A   Yup, you guessed it—Andrew "Badass" Jackson.

Q   Who is the only U.S. president to have been wounded while fighting in the Civil War?

A   Rutherford B. Hayes. And he wasn't wounded just once—he was wounded four separate times.

Q   Which four U.S. presidents were assassinated while in office?

A   Abraham Lincoln, James Garfield, William McKinley, and John F. Kennedy. Hey, you knew that Garfield and McKinley were presidents, right?

Q   Which six U.S. presidents survived assassination attempts while in office?

A   Andrew Jackson, Theodore Roosevelt, Franklin Roosevelt, Harry Truman, Gerald Ford, and Ronald Reagan.

Q   Which U.S. president served the shortest term in office?

A   William Henry Harrison. He died of pneumonia on his thirty-second day in office.

Q Who is the only U.S. president who didn't speak English as a first language?

A Martin van Buren. He was raised speaking Dutch. Interestingly, he was also the first president to be a U.S. citizen—all previous presidents were born before the American Revolution and were technically British subjects.

Q Who was the first U.S. president to appear in film?

A William McKinley. His inauguration ceremony in 1897 was the first to be captured on film. (Were you thinking it was Ronald Reagan in *Bedtime for Bonzo*? C'mon, admit it, that's what you were thinking.)

Q Besides being president, what do Ronald Reagan, George H.W. Bush, Bill Clinton, and Barack Obama have in common?

A All are left-handed (or ambidextrous, in the case of Reagan).

Q Which president appears on the $100,000 bill?

A Not a trick question! Bills in $100,000 denominations were used in the 1930s by the U.S. Treasury for internal transactions and were never publically circulated. The bills still exist and are considered legal tender if you can get your hands on one. The presidential face on the note belongs to Woodrow Wilson.

Q Which U.S. president had a pet dog named Satan while living in the White House?

A John Adams.

Q Which U.S. president owned two tiger cubs?

A Martin van Buren.

Q Which U.S. president's dog was named Fido?

A Abraham Lincoln.

Q Which U.S. president kept two opossums in the White House, named Mr. Reciprocity and Mr. Protection?

A Benjamin Harrison. How dope is that!

Q Which U.S. president owned a brown bear named Jonathan Edwards?

A Teddy Roosevelt.

Q Which U.S. president allowed alligators to roam the White House?

A Herbert Hoover. His son kept two pet alligators that were sometimes allowed to wander the halls of the White House.

TRUE OR FALSE? The treasurer of Alabama is named Young Boozer.

TRUE.

Note to the parents of Young Boozer: Um, what the hell were you ~~drinking~~ thinking when you named your son Young Boozer?

TRUE OR FALSE? Krystal Ball ran for U.S. Congress from Virginia, but her campaign was derailed when photos surfaced of her at a holiday party dressed as sexy Santa, kissing a dildo attached to her husband's nose (Rudolph, is that you?) and leading him on a leash.

TRUE.

And with a name like that, she should have seen it coming.

TRUE OR FALSE? Frank Schmuck ran for public office in Arizona under the motto "Team Schmuck!"

TRUE.

And he wasn't being ironic. Note that Schmuck defines TEAM as an acronym for Together Everyone Achieves More. Translation: More Schmuck! Go team!

TRUE OR FALSE? Janelle Lawless became a circuit judge specifically so that Reuters could write headlines about her such as "Lawless Circuit Judge Strikes Down Arkansas Marriage Amendment."

FALSE.

Janelle Lawless no doubt became a judge for other reasons. But still, extra points for a judge named Lawless.

TRUE OR FALSE? British politician Mark Reckless missed an important vote because he was too drunk.

TRUE.

It's sad when your name becomes your destiny.

TRUE OR FALSE? If Adolf Hitler had been born twelve years earlier, he would have been known as Adolf Schicklgruber.

TRUE.

Hitler's father, Alois Schicklgruber, changed his name to Alois Hitler in 1877; Adolf was born in 1889.

TRUE OR FALSE? Adolf Hitler was nominated for a Nobel Peace Prize in 1939.

TRUE.

The nomination was meant as a satirical comment—but hey, satire or not, it just doesn't look good to nominate Hitler for a Nobel Peace Prize.

TRUE OR FALSE? Adolf Hitler wanted to use a bomb hidden inside chocolate to assassinate Britain's prime minister at the time, Winston Churchill.

TRUE.

Apparently the idea of a chocolate-covered bomb seemed like a good idea to the dentist-hating Hitler.

TRUE OR FALSE? Adolf Hitler snorted cocaine, injected bull semen into his blood stream, farted continuously, and had chronic bad breath.

TRUE.

No wonder his long-term companion, Eva Braun, attempted suicide twice.

TRUE OR FALSE? The Mormon Church posthumously baptized Adolf Hitler in 1993.

TRUE.

Note to the Mormon Church: Living or dead, it's just plain weird to baptize Adolf Hitler.

TRUE OR FALSE? Adolf Hitler and the Nazis killed more people than Joseph Stalin and his Soviet regime.

FALSE.

Hitler and the Nazis killed millions of people, to be sure. But if you include civilians in the death count, historians now believe that Stalin and the Soviets are responsible for more deaths through purges, executions, mass murders, forced migrations, famines, and genocides. It's a dubious honor no matter how you do the math.

TRUE OR FALSE? Stalin attempted to assassinate Yugoslavian leader Josip Tito more than twenty-two times.

TRUE.

> And it's not a great testament to the prowess of Soviet assassins. Tito lived until 1980.

TRUE OR FALSE? When Stalin suffered a fatal stroke in 1953, his doctors treated him with leeches.

TRUE.

TRUE OR FALSE? Saparmurat Niyazov, the former and deceased dictator of Turkmenistan, ordered that the months of the year be renamed after members of his family.

TRUE.

Did you know?

> Besides renaming the months after his family, Turkmenistan's former dictator also banned lip-synching at concerts and outlawed all performances of opera, ballet, and the circus.
>
> Holiday in Turkmenistan, anybody?

TRUE OR FALSE? The first time he played golf, North Korea's former dictator, Kim Jong-il, had five holes-in-one for a 38-under-par round.

TRUE.

> If you believe Kim Jong-il's official biography.

TRUE OR FALSE? The first time Kim Jong-il went bowling, he scored a perfect 300.

TRUE.

The dude clearly abides.

TRUE OR FALSE? The current year in North Korea is 104.

TRUE.

North Korea's official calendar is based on the year Kim Jong-il was born, not on when that Jesus dude was born.

TRUE OR FALSE? North Korea is the world's happiest nation.

FALSE.

North Korea came in second place (behind China) according to a recent happiness study commissioned by—wait for it—North Korea!

TRUE OR FALSE? American citizens have risked their lives defecting to North Korea.

TRUE.

And yeah, you read that correctly—defecting *to* not *from* North Korea. The most famous example is James Joseph Dresnok, an American soldier who defected in 1962. He's still alive, living in North Korea's capital of Pyongyang. The television show *60 Minutes* featured an interview with Dresnok in 2007.

TRUE OR FALSE? Scientists from North Korea's History Institute discovered a unicorn's lair in 2012.

TRUE.

Apparently it was the lair of a unicorn ridden a few thousand years ago by a revered king of ancient Korea.

TRUE OR FALSE? Marijuana is not considered an illicit drug in North Korea.

_____

TRUE.

And really, when you think about it, it explains a lot about North Korea.

TRUE OR FALSE? North Korea's "three generations of punishment" policy means that, for crimes against the central government such as trying to flee the country, you can be sent to a prison camp. And the two subsequent generations of your family born in the camp will be forced to live and die there too.

_____

TRUE.

At this point, crazy monomaniacal dictators are no longer amusing.

TRUE OR FALSE? The moon is governed by the United Nations.

_____

MOSTLY TRUE.

The ratified 1979 Moon Treaty stipulates that the moon—and all celestial bodies in our solar system—should not be used for military purposes and must be preserved for the benefit of the international community. The United Nations retains some jurisdiction over the moon, in the sense that all activities on the moon must conform to the United Nations Charter.

TRUE OR FALSE? You can purchase land on the moon.

_____

TRUE.

The website Lunarembassy.com sells acreage on the moon and other planets within our solar system. One acre with a view on Mercury goes for as little as $19.99. However—and it's a large however—there's no guarantee your deed of ownership will be recognized by anybody that matters.

1. Timocracy
2. Minarchism
3. Ochlocracy
4. Confederacy
5. Plutocracy
6. Exilarchy
7. Kleptocracy
8. Diarchy
9. Noocracy
10. Demarchy

A. Government by the wealthy

B. Only property owners may participate in government

C. Government exists to make its leaders more wealthy and powerful at the expense of the general population

D. Government by two joint heads of state

E. Government's only role is to protect residents from aggression, theft, and fraud

F. Government run by the power of the collective human brain

G. Government by mob rule

H. Form of rule by an honorific leader who wields influence over a religious sect or ethnic group (think: the Dalai Lama)

I. Government of limited powers, joining together independent states or territories that retain all authority except in matters specifically assigned to the central government

J. Government by people randomly selected from a pool of eligible citizens

ANSWERS

1B, 2E, 3G, 4I, 5A, 6H, 7C, 8D, 9F, 10J

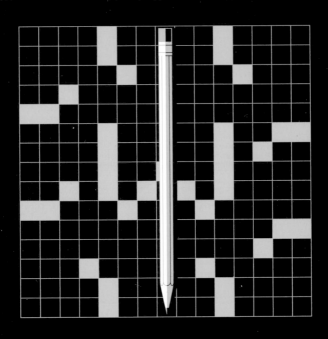

WORD
PLAY

Q If shepherds herd sheep and goatherds herd goats, do gooseherds herd geese?

A Yes. And if you happen to own geese, you're a gozzard.

Q What are the plurals of goose and mongoose?

A Geese and mongooses, of course.

Q What are the plurals of deer, moose, and sheep?

A Deer, moose, and sheep. Duh!

Q What's the plural of octopus?

A Octopuses. Some dictionaries accept the less common octopodes, which acknowledges the word's Greek origins. What about octopi? Never! Friends don't let friends use Latin pluralization suffixes on Greek root words.

Q What are the singular forms of dice and lice?

A Die and louse.

Q What are the plurals of schema and index?

A Schemata and indices. That said, the incorrect "schemas" and "indexes" are becoming more common in American usage, because we're lazy louts who don't pay attention in grammar school.

Q What are the plurals of memo and potato?

A Memos and potatoes. There's no good reason why some o-ending words are pluralized with "oes" while others simply add "os." But get it wrong at your own peril; just ask former Vice President Dan "Potatoe" Quayle.

Q What are the singular forms of pajamas, shorts, jeans, tights, trousers, and glasses?

A Trick question. These words do not have accepted singular forms. They properly exist only in the plural. Clothes can be annoying like that.

Q What are the plurals of half, calf, and elf?

A Halves, calves, and elves. (Don't call them elfs—it only makes them angry.)

Q What is an ogdoad?

A A group or set of eight things.

Q Is it "tow the line" or "toe the line"?

A Toe the line. This idiom is not about pulling with ropes and chains; it's about conforming and standing at roll call with your toe on the mark.

Q If "off" means to deactivate, what happens when the alarm goes off?

A It wakes you up.

Q Does "left" mean remaining, or to have departed?

A Both. The dog left the house, so the cat is the only animal left inside.

Q Does "out" mean visible or invisible?

A Both. The light went out when the moon was out.

Q Is it "chomping at the bit" or "champing at the bit"?

A Horses don't impatiently chomp on their bits, they champ. Metaphorically speaking, humans do too.

Q Does a ne'er-do-well get his "just desserts" or his "just deserts"?

A The latter. "Desert" in this case is an archaic word—in modern usage, it doesn't exist outside of this phrase—and means "that which you deserve." Just desserts are best left to your local cake shop.

Q What are the only four words in modern English that end in "dous"?

A Tremendous, horrendous, stupendous, and hazardous.

Q What are the only two words in modern English that end in "gry"?

A Angry and hungry. No credit for variants of hungry and angry, nor for weird ancient words that nobody actually uses (we're talking about you, bungry and braggry).

Q What words rhyme with "orange"?

A Though many have tried, no words rhyme with orange. It's the same sad case with the rhymeless words silver, elbow, galaxy, and rhythm. Wasp, purple, and month are also hard to rhyme.

Q Which is smaller, a drib or a drab?

A Neither. Both mean small or negligible amounts. Drib is possibly a shortening of driblet, which is less than a drop. Drab means a small amount of money. Both are archaic and don't exist nowadays outside of this idiomatic phrase.

Q Decimate or obliterate—which is more destructive?

A Technically speaking the more destructive word is obliterate. Decimate was coined by the Romans, who used it to mean that one in every ten members of a mutinous army unit would be killed as a way to dissuade other would-be mutineers. On the other hand, to obliterate is to destroy utterly.

Q Moron, imbecile, or idiot—which is worse?

A In the early twentieth century, psychologists used these words technically to distinguish people with IQs at the low end of the scale. Morons (IQ range of 51 to 70) were a step ahead of imbeciles (IQ range of 26 to 50) and two steps ahead of idiots (IQ range of 0 to 25).

Q What century was the word "earthling" first used—the sixteenth, seventeenth, or eighteenth??

A In the 1590s, the Old English word "yrþling" (earth + -ling) meant both a ploughman and an "inhabitant of the earth." So the sixteenth century wins! The word's first use in science fiction was in Robert Heinlein's 1949 novel *Red Planet*.

Q Which word is oldest—hairdresser, guitar, spaceship, or cocktail?

A Guitar—and by a long shot! It was first recorded in the 1620s. The next-oldest word is hairdresser, from the 1770s. Cocktail was first used in 1806, and spaceship dates from 1894.

Did you know?

The word "dictionary" was coined by the English in 1220. John of Garland wrote a book called *Dictionarius* to help readers master Latin diction. The first dictionaries were English-language glossaries of French or Latin words with their English equivalents.

Q When were the words "nerd" and "geek" first used?

A Dr. Seuss is credited with the first use of "nerd" in print, from his 1950 book *If I Ran the Zoo*. The word "geek'" has a longer and more colorful history—it comes from the German word "geck," which means fool. Circus "geek shows" featured wild performances; the term "geek" itself became part of American pop culture thanks to William Gresham's 1946 novel *Nightmare Alley*, which is possibly the finest pulp-fiction novel ever written about circus life. Geeks with glasses and pocket protectors didn't exist until the 1980s.

Q What do funambulists do?

A They walk on tightropes.

Q What do noctambulists do?

A They walk in their sleep.

Q What does a famulus do?

A Assists magicians during performances.

Q What does a karateka do?

A Performs karate.

Q What does an ecdysiast do?

A Performs striptease.

Q What's a weirkeeper?

A Somebody who manages fish traps.

Q What does it take to become a hobbler?

A A boat. Hobblers tow boats on rivers and canals.

Q What does a mudlark do?

A Scours rivers at low tide in search of valuables buried in the mud.

Q What's a haberdasher?

A Somebody who deals in men's clothing.

Be careful with mountweazels. If you're holding one, you're holding something that doesn't exist but can still get you into serious trouble. What is it?

Mountweazels are spurious entries or fake works used to catch copyright cheats. The name honors Lillian Virginia Mountweazel, a famous photographer who appeared in the New Columbia Encyclopedia's 1975 edition. The problem, of course, is that Lillian Virginia Mountweazel never existed. She was created specifically to catch fraudsters. Other words that don't exist—but are sometimes included in print to catch plagiarists—include esquivalence, jungftak, and zzxjoanw.

You can thank the Germans for having a word that describes these fakeries: *Nihilartikel*. It's formed from the Latin word "nihil" (nothing) and the German word "Artikel" (article).

Q What's special about the 1939 novel *Gadsby*?

A It does not contain a single word with the letter "e." That's no small feat in a fifty-thousand-word book. It also means that it can only be two, four, or six o'clock in the novel. And no, the novel should never be available as an e-book.

Q What's the longest palindrome in the *Oxford English Dictionary*?

A Tattarrattat. Coined by James Joyce in his novel *Ulysses* for a knock on the door.

Q What's the longest palindrome in any language?

A *Saippuakivikauppias*. It's nineteen letters long and means "soap seller" in Finnish.

➡ WHAT DO THESE THREE SENTENCES HAVE IN COMMON?

A A mad boxer shot a quick, gloved jab to the jaw of his dizzy opponent.

B Five or six big jet planes zoomed quickly by the tower.

C Now is the time for all quick brown dogs to jump over the lazy lynx.

ANSWER

They each use every letter in the alphabet.

Q What is pneumonoultramicroscopicsilicovolcanokoniosis?

A The longest made-up word in the *Oxford English Dictionary*.

 **Did you know?**

"The sixth sick sheik's sixth sheep is sick" is said to be the toughest tongue twister in the English language.

Q What is floccinaucinihilipilification?

A The longest real word (29 letters) in the *Oxford English Dictionary*.

Q What is honorificabilitudinitatibus?

A The longest word (27 letters) to appear in Shakespeare's work, from *Love's Labor Lost*.

Q What words are illegal to speak on radio and television in the United States?

A None. The Federal Communications Commission (FCC) has never published a list of banned words. It is widely assumed that comedian George Carlin's infamous list of seven "filthy" words could get you into administrative hot water with the FCC. Even this is not certain, however, given that the U.S. Supreme Court declined to rule on a case involving Carlin's stand-up routine that was broadcast on radio. It's also uncertain given that the FCC's rule against "fleeting expletives" was ruled unconstitutional in 2010.

Q What are George Carlin's seven "filthy" words?

A Shit, piss, fuck, cunt, cocksucker, motherfucker, tits. These were performed in a stand-up routine by Carlin in 1972 (he was arrested during one of his performances). Comedian Lenny Bruce was also arrested, in 1966, for publicly speaking the seven words above, as well as for adding "ass" and "balls" into the mix.

Go Hang a Salami, I'm a Lasagna Hog

Some of the best palindromes ever:

- A man, a plan, a canal. Panama!

- A man, a plan, a cat, a ham, a yak, a yam, a hat, a canal. Panama!

- Never odd or even

- Madam, in Eden I'm Adam

- Was it a rat I saw?

- Was it a bar or a bat I saw?

- Yo, banana boy

- Able was I ere I saw Elba

- Dr. Awkward

- Lived on decaf, faced no devil

- As I pee, sir, I see Pisa

- A Toyota! Race fast, safe car! A Toyota!

- Live not on evil

- God saw I was dog

Scrabble

Q

Define the following legitimate two-letter Scrabble words:

1 aa	**6** ai	**11** as
2 ab	**7** al	**12** at
3 ae	**8** am	**13** aw
4 ag	**9** an	**14** ax
5 ah	**10** ar	**15** ay

ANSWERS

1 aa is rough, cindery lava

2 ab is an abdominal muscle

3 ae means one

4 ag means agricultural

5 ah is a variant of aah

6 ai is a three-toed sloth

7 al is an East Indian tree

8 am as in "I am"

9 an as in "an abomination"

10 ar stands for the letter "r"

11 as means to the same degree

12 at as in the preposition

13 aw is used to express disbelief

14 ax is the chopping kind

15 ay is a variant of "aye"

Q How many two-letter Scrabble words exist starting with the letter "z"?

A One. It's the word "za," and you'll be annoyed to learn it means "pizza."

Q How many three-letter Scrabble words exist starting with the letter "z"?

A Fifteen, according to the *Official Scrabble Players' Dictionary*. They are zag, zap, zas, zax, zed, zee, zek, zep, zig, zin, zip, zit, zoa, zoo, and zuz.

Q What would a Scotsman do with a spurtle?

A Stir porridge. It's a type of wooden stirring tool for the kitchen.

Q What would a German do with a *Backpfeifengesicht*?

A Slap them around. *Backpfeifengesicht* is the German way of saying somebody needs a slap in the head.

Q If a German says *Vorgestern*, what day are they referring to?

A The day before yesterday.

Q If a German says *Übermorgen*, what day are they referring to?

A The day after tomorrow. Bless the Germans for having words to clearly express both concepts.

Q If a German sign says *Geschwindigkeitsbeschränkungen*, what does it mean?

A It's a long way of saying "speed limit."

Q If a German is a *Handschuhschneeballwerfer*, what are they likely wearing on their hands?

A Gloves. The word means "person who wears gloves to throw snowballs," with connotations of being a coward.

Q What does the German word *Rindfleischetikettierungsüberwachungsaufgabenübertragungsgesetz* refer to?

A It's a law dictating how to label beef correctly. The fact that the law was repealed in 2010 doesn't make the word any less awesome.

Q What does a German store called a *Haarschmuckfachgeschäft* sell?

A Hair ornaments, of course.

Q What does a German mean when saying *"Er ist dick"*?

A Not what you think. The phrase means "He is fat."

Q What does the German word *Fahrtwind* mean?

A Air turbulence. Not the smelly kind.

Q How many anagrams can you make from Clint Eastwood's name?

A More than 115,000, including "Old West action," "old instate cow," and "Taco Idle Wonts."

Washington Crossing the Delaware

What is unique about David Shulman's 1936 sonnet, "Washington Crossing the Delaware"?

A hard, howling, tossing water scene.
Strong tide was washing hero clean.
"How cold!" Weather stings as in anger.
O Silent night shows war ace danger!

The cold waters swashing on in rage.
Redcoats warn slow his hint engage.
When star general's action wish'd "Go!"
He saw his ragged continentals row.

Ah, he stands—sailor crew went going.
And so this general watches rowing.
He hastens—winter again grows cold.
A wet crew gain Hessian stronghold.

George can't lose war with's hands in;
He's astern—so go alight, crew, and win!

ANSWER

Each of its fourteen lines is an anagram of the sonnet's title. And it rhymes!

1	absquatulate	A	One who eats frogs
2	adelphepothia	B	A happy ending in a story
3	batrachophagous	C	To leave someplace abruptly
4	coprolalia	D	Involuntary and repetitive use of obscene language
5	adoxography	E	Skilled writing on an unimportant subject
6	eucatastrophe	F	An incestuous desire for one's sister
7	logomachy	G	An argument about words

ANSWERS

1C, 2F, 3A, 4D, 5E, 6B, 7G

144

Q Where does the phrase "happy as a clam" come from?

A It makes more sense when you hear the original version— "happy as a clam at high water," when the clam's predators are held at bay.

Q Besides corn, what other food items can you "shuck"?

A Shellfish, such as oysters and clams.

Did you know?

People once pronounced the "k" in words like knight, knowledge, and knob. In Old English, the silent "k'" was not silent. It's the same with words like "gnat" and "gnome"—in ye olde days, the "g" was pronounced.

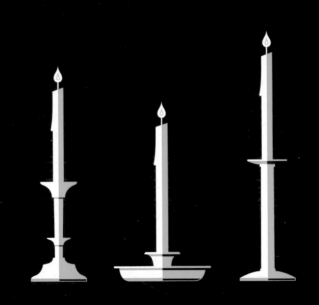

RELIGION

Religion

Q What's the world's most popular religion?

A Christianity, claiming roughly 32 percent of the world's population.

Q What's the world's second-most popular religion?

A Islam, boasting roughly 23 percent of the world's population.

Q What's the third-largest religious group worldwide?

A Unaffiliated. More than one in six people around the globe profess a spiritual belief but are not affiliated with any official religion. Amen.

Q What's your likely religion if your goal in life is to attain self-realization and have your soul occupy bodies with ever-increasing abilities?

A Hinduism, the world's fourth-largest religion.

Q Buddhism, Jainism, and Sikhism were inspired by what religion?

A Hinduism.

>>>>>>>>>>>> **Did you know?** <<<<<<<<<<<<

Jews comprise just 0.02 percent of the world's population—that's a mere 14 million adherents worldwide.

TRUE OR FALSE? According to the Bible, Adam and Eve were kicked out of the Garden of Eden because Adam ate the forbidden fruit from the Tree of Knowledge.

FALSE.

It wasn't eating from the Tree of Knowledge that got Adam ejected from Eden. Rather God was worried that, once Adam knew right from wrong, he would next eat from the Tree of Life, making him immortal. God didn't want any competition on the immortal front.

TRUE OR FALSE? Adam died when he was 930 years old.

TRUE.

According to the Bible, he also fathered a son at the randy age of 130.

TRUE OR FALSE? According to the Bible, men should not shave any part of their heads or beards.

TRUE.

And don't get a tattoo as a way of worshiping the dead—that's frowned upon.

Name that Religion

Q

Match the descriptions with their respective religions.

1 You believe in tantric sex. You revere cows. You believe in reincarnation and frequently worship phallic objects in a temple.

2 People should behave honorably in whatever role they have in society to promote harmony, prosperity, and happiness. No gods. No afterlife.

3 No self. No soul. No ultimate reality. You believe suffering permeates all existence. Once you die you are reborn or you attain enlightenment (no pressure!). Ultimate goal is to escape the cycle of rebirth.

4 You believe in one God. You live in a balanced, worldly manner. Your ultimate goal is to be absorbed into God. There is no heaven or hell. If you're a man, you wear a turban in public.

5 No gods. Man is the master of everything. You're a self-sufficient socialist. You practice with religious fervor despite living in an atheist police state.

6 Your religion was founded by a nineteenth-century nobleman from Tehran and today has its headquarters in Israel. You believe in one God and one human race. All religions are the same and represent stages in the revelation of God's will. Your main gripe with the modern world? Most people cannot accept the fact of their oneness.

7 One of the oldest religions in the world. And one of the first monotheist religions. Heaven and hell are real. Christianity and Judaism borrowed many of your concepts. Only 200,000 people worship this religion today. Freddy Mercury of the band Queen was a strict adherent.

8 You believe Blacks are the chosen people of God, but colonization and the slave trade have made it impossible to achieve your destiny. One day you will return to Africa. You don't drink alcohol or cut your hair. Smoking marijuana and chanting increase your spirituality.

ANSWERS

1 Hinduism

2 Confucianism

3 Buddhism

4 Sikhism

5 Juche

6 Bahai'

7 Zoroastrianism

8 Rastafari

TRUE OR FALSE? According to the Bible, if your wife defends your life in a fight by grabbing your attacker's genitals, you should cut off your wife's hand and have no pity on her.

TRUE.

Better for you to die unjustly than for your lawful wife to defend you with a below-the-belt maneuver. Just don't tell Gloria Steinem.

TRUE OR FALSE? According to the Bible, if you want to sleep with your brother's wife, it's better to masturbate—or better yet, to pull out early and to ejaculate on the ground, in order to avoid getting her pregnant.

TRUE.

TRUE OR FALSE? According to the Bible, if you're bald and a large group of boys jeer at you and shout "Get out of here, baldy," you should lay a curse on them. At which point two female bears will come out of the woods and maul the boys.

TRUE.

So true.

TRUE OR FALSE? According to the Bible, if your testicles have been crushed, do not attempt to join the Assembly of God (e.g., a church).

TRUE.

You will not be welcome.

TRUE OR FALSE? According to the Bible, if robbers come to your house while you're having guests, it's better to offer up your two virgin daughters to the robbers than for your guests to come to any harm.

TRUE.

And Gloria Steinem's head just exploded.

TRUE OR FALSE? According to the Bible, you should not breed two kinds of cattle, sow your fields with two kinds of seed, or wear cotton-polyester blends.

TRUE.

Why no cotton-polyester blends? Apparently you should not wear garments made of two materials mixed together.

TRUE OR FALSE? The proper way to seal a deal in the Bible is to exchange sandals.

TRUE.

But annoying if your large feet don't fit comfortably into your new business partner's smaller footwear.

TRUE OR FALSE? According to the Bible, eagles, vultures, buzzards, crows, ostriches, hawks, seagulls, owls, pelicans, storks, herons, and bats are disgusting, and you are forbidden to eat any of them.

TRUE.

Ditto for all winged insects *except* locusts, grasshoppers, and crickets, which you may eat—and *mmmm*, aren't they delicious!

TRUE OR FALSE? According to the Bible, if you want to be a priest you should not be blind or lame, have a disfigured face, have one leg shorter than the other, or be a hunchback or a dwarf, and your testicles should be in good shape.

TRUE.

No hunchback priests need apply.

TRUE OR FALSE? According to the Bible, gay people should just be killed.

MOSTLY TRUE.

Leviticus 20:13 says "If a man lies with a male as with a woman, both of them have committed an abomination; they shall surely be put to death; their blood is upon them." God loves a sinner, but he's not a huge fan of the sin itself.

TRUE OR FALSE? The Bible forbids Jews from consuming milk with meat.

FALSE.

The Bible simply says, "Don't boil a young goat in its mother's milk." Religious scholars have interpreted this as an injunction not to consume milk and meat together.

TRUE OR FALSE? The Bible commands observant Jews to wear skullcaps, or yarmulkes, as a sign of faith.

FALSE.

Wearing yarmulkes is not mentioned in the Bible.

TRUE OR FALSE? On the eve of Yom Kippur, some observant Jews swing live chickens over their heads three times to atone for their sins. Their sins are transferred to the chickens, which are then slaughtered.

TRUE.

It's called *kaparos*.

TRUE OR FALSE? Ultra-orthodox Jews have sex through a hole in a sheet.

FALSE.

It's a myth based on the fact that ultra-orthodox boys and girls are educated separately and have little interaction until their marriage night.

⫸⫸⫸⫸⫸⫸⫸⫸ **Did you know?** ⫷⫷⫷⫷⫷⫷⫷⫷

Because it's not permitted to tear things on *Shabbat* (the day of rest, beginning Friday at sunset and ending the following evening after nightfall), kosher toilet paper comes pre-cut into sheets. Entire businesses have grown up around this religious prohibition. Here's just one example of an honest-to-goodness marketing slogan of Shabbat-friendly toilet paper available online:

"No need to pre-tear toilet paper! No awkward reaching for tissue on back of tank. Why waste money on expensive facial tissue?"

TRUE OR FALSE? Religious Jews believe in Jesus.

TRUE.

> They believe Jesus was a prophet. They do not believe Jesus was the Messiah. (Spoiler alert: false Messiah!)

TRUE OR FALSE? Jews for Jesus is an evangelical Christian organization with a mission to convert Jews to a Christian way of life.

TRUE.

> The Jews for Jesus mission statement is, "We exist to make the messiahship of Jesus an unavoidable issue to our Jewish people worldwide." Very clever marketing on the part of conservative Christians, *non*?

TRUE OR FALSE? Religious Jews don't believe in an afterlife.

MOSTLY TRUE.

> There is no official Jewish conception of the afterlife—only passing references in the Bible to hell-like realms which lack the Christian notions of punishment and judgment.

TRUE OR FALSE? More than 60 percent of Americans think the story of Noah's Ark—guy builds boat, guy rescues two of every animal on earth from a global flood, guy and animals survive flood—is literal truth.

TRUE.

Top 3 Mean Bible Quotes

1 "May the Lord bless everyone who beats your children against the rocks!" (Psalm 137:9). In other words: It's OK to murder babies.

2 "Women who claim to love God should do helpful things for others, and they should learn by being quiet and paying attention. They should be silent and not be allowed to teach or to tell men what to do." (1 Timothy 2:10-12). In other words: Women move to the back of the bus and do what the menfolk tell you.

3 "It's better to dwell alone in the desert than at home with a nagging, complaining wife." (Proverbs 21:19). Especially if all she wants to do is talk about her day and make you feel bad for drinking a beer in front of the television.

TRUE OR FALSE? More than 46 percent of Americans believe God created humans in their present form, at one time, within the last 10,000 years.

TRUE.

TRUE OR FALSE? God has commanded Mormons to avoid coffee and tea.

T R U E.

TRUE OR FALSE? Mormons believe that Jesus Christ visited the Americas.

T R U E.

The Book of Mormon is meant to be contemporaneous with the Bible. After Jesus's resurrection, Mormon scripture says he visited (as in, descending from Heaven in a white robe) the peoples of the Americas. Jesus, welcome to Mississippi!

TRUE OR FALSE? Mormons believe the Garden of Eden was located in northern Missouri.

T R U E.

Mormon founder Joseph Smith had a revelation from God about the location of Eden during a trip through Missouri in 1838.

TRUE OR FALSE? People of African descent (e.g., every Black person on the planet) were barred from becoming Mormon priests until 1978.

T R U E.

In 1978, Mormons recognized the impossibility of opening a temple in Brazil with their strict racial policies for priesthood. So they relented and allowed Blacks to become Mormon priests.

TRUE OR FALSE? Mormons believe there are multiple universes, with multiple Gods.

TRUE.

Mormons pioneered the notion of "multiverses." Multiple Gods exist, according to church doctrine, each with his own universe (and yes, the Mormon god is clearly a "he"). Added bonus? Humans who obtain the highest level of heaven can become gods, too.

Q Who said, "Writing for a penny a word is ridiculous. If a man really wants to make a million dollars, the best way would be to start his own religion."

A L. Ron Hubbard, the founder of Scientology.

Did you know?

L. Ron Hubbard published a self-help book in 1950 called *Dianetics*, which became an immediate best-seller as well as the defining text of the nascent Scientology movement.

The idea behind *Dianetics* is that your mind is filled with traumatic memories called "engrams," which are the source of nightmares and insecurities. Scientologists strive to free engrams of their painful qualities, leaving a person "clear."

Q How many countries consider Scientology to be a cult or sect?

A At least three: Israel, France, and Chile. Many more countries have ruled that Scientology is neither a religion nor a religious community.

Q Where was the Church of Scientology officially founded?

A Los Angeles, California, in 1954.

Q What do you call the paramilitary wing of the Church of Scientology?

A Sea Org, or Sea Organization. This is the church's private naval force, originally based in the 1960s on four vessels in the Mediterranean. Sea Org members sign a billion-year contract and occupy high-level posts within the church. Most activities are now land based, though a vessel called *Freewinds*, sailed and staffed by Sea Org members, continues to operate in Caribbean waters as "a perfect religious retreat dedicated to enabling one to devote his full attention to spiritual growth."

Q What do Sonny Bono, Kirsty Allie, Nancy Cartwright (voice of Bart Simpson), Chick Corea, Tom Cruise, Isaac Hayes, Juliette Lewis, Priscilla Presley, Danny Masterson, Giovanni Ribisi, John Travolta, and Greta Van Susteren all have in common?

A They are all members of the Church of Scientology.

Q What did actor Danny Masterson say when asked why he'd want to be a Scientologist in a 2005 interview with *Spin* magazine?

A "I'd be a flaming crackhead if I didn't study Scientology." Which is an insult to crackheads, if you think about it.

Q According to Scientology doctrine, why did Xenu bring billions of people to Earth, gather them near volcanoes, and drop hydrogen bombs on them?

A It's complicated. About 75 million years ago, Xenu was the evil dictator of the Galactic Confederacy. It's unclear why he did what he did. But the souls of all those dead people were forced to watch a "three-D, super colossal motion picture" that gave them false memories of Jesus and all the world religions. These misguided souls now negatively affect everyone who has not had them removed by the Church of Scientology. Hey Masterson—what was that about crack heads? If this makes any sense to you, it's only because you *are* a Scientologist.

Q Is it possible to believe in no god *and* to be spiritual?

A Yes. More than a quarter of atheists claim to be spiritual and believe in a universal spirit. A majority of atheists also claim to feel a deep connection with nature (damn hippies). Just don't call it God.

Top 5 Joke Religions

It's easy to make fun of Christians, Jews, and Muslims. Buddhists and Mormons are equally easy to laugh at. And then there are religions that are so plain weird that jokes kinda, sorta miss the point.

1 The Universe People. They live in the Czech Republic and believe that ancient nonearthly beings operate a fleet of spaceships orbiting the Earth. The Universe People followers are waiting to be transported into another dimension. Fair enough.

2 Nuwaubianism. It's a loose term referring to the religion founded by Dwight York, a Black supremacist leader and convicted child molester (he's currently in jail for 135 years). Some things the Nuwaubianists believe: All humans have seven clones living on different parts of the planet, humans were bred on Mars as part of a Homo erectus breeding program gone awry, and famed scientist Nikola Tesla was born on the planet Venus. Amen.

3 Bhagwan Shree Rajneesh. He was an India-born mystic who eventually settled in Oregon in the 1980s. The group's claims to religious fame? Preaching that Rolls-Royces were a sign of holiness (Bhagwan Rashneesh owned dozens of them) and trying to poison nonbelievers by introducing salmonella into salad bars in several Oregon fast-food restaurants.

4 World Church of the Creator. It's a white separatist
   movement advocating a white-only religion called
   Creativity. Ironically, despite their name, group
   members do not believe in God. They are atheists!

5 Heaven's Gate. A cult founded by Marshall Applewhite.
   His followers believed that once they were free of their
   earthly bodies, a spaceship would take them away to
   a celestial paradise. Clearly the 1997 appearance of
   the Hale-Bopp comet was a sign their spaceship had
   arrived. In March of that year, thirty-six members
   of the cult were found dead in a mass suicide. Their
   bags were packed. They all wore running shoes and
   matching uniforms with patches that said "Heaven's
   Gate Away Team." They all had a $5 bill and a roll of
   quarters in their pockets. You couldn't make this stuff
   up if you tried.

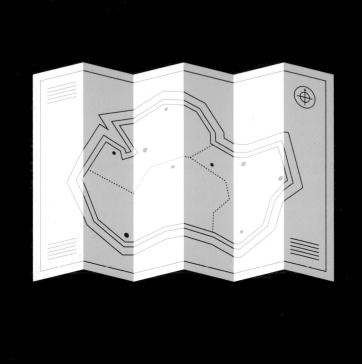

CITIES

COUNTRIES

Cities & Countries

Q Which is larger, a hamlet or a burg?

A Burg. Hamlets are small settlements with enclosed land or pastures. Burgs are larger, fortified settlements.

Q Which is larger, a village or town?

A Town. Villages have multiple families and clusters of buildings used for different purposes (barns, storehouses, etc.). In Europe, villages often gain their status by virtue of having a church. Towns are basically large villages with some type of local government or council. Typically they also have craftspeople specializing in a trade or commercial pursuit.

Q Which is larger, a town or borough?

A Trick question. In most jurisdictions borough is just a different name for a town. Both are distinct from cities, which in the U.S. are legal entities (called "incorporated cities") empowered to provide services to local residents. In ye olde days in Western Europe, having a cathedral was a sure sign you lived in a city.

>>>>>>>>>>>>>> **Did you know?** <<<<<<<<<<<<<<

In the nineteenth century fewer than 3 percent of the world's population lived in cities. By the mid-twentieth century more than 83 cities had populations greater than 1 million. In the early twenty-first century, the figure jumped to 470, with an additional 380 cities clocking in with populations greater than 500,000.

Q What's the difference between a city and a megacity?

A Megacities are cities with one specific twist: More than 10 million people must live there. At last count, twenty-six cities worldwide had earned the status of "megacity."

Q Which country has the most megacities?

A China. Shanghai, Beijing, Guangzhou-Foshan, and Shenzhen all have populations greater than 10 million.

➤ AFTER CHINA, WHICH TWO COUNTRIES FROM THE FOLLOWING LIST ARE HOME TO THE GREATEST NUMBER OF MEGACITIES?

A Brazil   E Japan

B Egypt   F Pakistan

C India   G Philippines

D Indonesia   H United States

ANSWER

India and Japan, both with three. India has Delhi, Mumbai, and Kolkata; Japan has Tokyo-Yokohama, Osaka-Kobe-Kyoto, and Nagoya.

Q   What is the world's most densely populated city?

A   Dhaka in Bangladesh, where 115,000 people live per square mile. That's a mere 240 square feet of living space per person.

Q   What's the world's most expensive city in which to live?

A   London. Rents in the British capital average £2,500 a month (approx. $4,100). How very uncivilized.

Q   What's the world's second-most expensive city in which to live?

A   Oslo, Norway. And you can bet that this is more of a supply problem than a demand problem. When's the last time you met somebody moving to Oslo?

Q   Of the world's major cities, which is the cheapest in which to live?

A   Kolkata, India.

➤ ON A RECENT LIST OF THE WORLD'S 10 UGLIEST CITIES, WHICH OF THE FOLLOWING CITIES WERE NOT INCLUDED?

A   Guatemala City, Guatemala   E   Houston, Texas

B   Mexico City, Mexico   F   Detroit, Michigan

C   Amman, Jordan   G   Baltimore, Maryland

D   Caracas, Venezuela   H   Sao Paulo, Brazil

ANSWER

   G. The rest of the cities all made the list.

➤ **WHAT ARE THE WORLD'S TOP FOUR MOST-HATED CITIES, ACCORDING TO A RECENT CNN POLL?**

A Melbourne, Australia

B Los Angeles, California

C Sydney, Australia

D Tijuana, Mexico

E Moscow, Russia

F Tegucigalpa, Honduras

G Buffalo, New York

H Paris, France

ANSWER

Tijuana (violence, pollution, crime), Melbourne (if you're from Sydney) or Sydney (if you're from Melbourne), and Paris (rude, rude, rude).

➤ **WHAT IS THE OFFICIAL SPORT OF MARYLAND?**

A Fencing

B Jousting

C Archery

D Hide and Seek

ANSWER

B

1	Paris	A	The Big Easy
2	Amsterdam	B	The Square Mile
3	New Orleans	C	Sin City
4	Seattle	D	Little Cuba
5	Rome	E	The Eternal City
6	Toronto	F	Athens of the North
7	Edinburgh	G	Emerald City
8	London	H	The Big Apple
9	Lisbon	I	City of Angels
10	Las Vegas	J	City of Light
11	New York City	K	The White City
12	Bangkok	L	The Big Toe
13	Los Angeles	M	Venice of the East
14	Miami	N	Venice of the North
15	Reno	O	The Biggest Little City

ANSWERS

1J, 2N, 3A, 4G, 5E, 6L, 7F, 8B, 9K, 10C, 11H, 12M, 13I, 14D, 15O

➤ **WHICH OF THE FOLLOWING CITIES HAS THE OLDEST SUBWAY SYSTEM?**

A Budapest

B London

C Glasgow

D Chicago

E New York City

F Paris

G Boston

ANSWER

B. London's Underground system is the world's oldest. It opened in 1863 between Paddington and Farringdon.

➤ **MATCH THE FOLLOWING STATES WITH THEIR OFFICIAL NICKNAMES.**

1	Delaware	A	Prairie State
2	Idaho	B	Pelican State
3	Illinois	C	The First State
4	Louisiana	D	Peace Garden State
5	North Dakota	E	Volunteer State
6	Tennessee	F	Gem State
7	Utah	G	Beehive State

ANSWERS

1C, 2F, 3A, 4B, 5D, 6E, 7G

Q What's the longest place name on Earth?

A Llanfairpwllgwyngyll in Wales. If that wasn't enough of a mouthful, the town's lesser-used official name is Llanfairpwllg-wyngyllgogerychwyrndrobwllllantysiliogogogogochuchaf.

Q And what is the meaning of that mouthful of a town name in Wales?

A St. Mary's Church in the hollow of the white hazel near the whirlpool of Llantysilio of the red cave.

Q What's the world's longest Internet domain name?

A www.llanfairpwllgwyngyllgogerychwyrndrobwllllantysil-iogogogogochuchaf.org.uk

Q What's the official name of the city of Los Angeles?

A El Pueblo de Nuestra Senora la Reina de los Angeles de Porciuncula. It's much simpler to call the locals "Angelenos."

Q What do you call an anonymous person in the United States?

A John or Jane Doe. Sometimes also John or Jane Roe (as in the famous Supreme Court case *Roe v. Wade*).

Q What do you call an average person in the United States?

A Average Joe, John Q. Public, Joe Blow, Joe Sixpack, or Joe Schmoe.

Q What do you call an average person in the United Kingdom?

A Fred or Joe Bloggs, John Smith, Joe or Jane Public, or A.N. Other.

Q What do you call an average person in Canada?
A G. Raymond, John Jones, or Jos Bleau.

Q What do you call an average person in Colombia?
A Pepito Pérez.

Q What do you call an average person in Lithuania?
A Vardenis Pavardenis.

Q What do you call an average person in Israel?
A Israel Israeli.

Q What do you call an average person in Nepal?
A Ram.

Q What do you call an average person in Nigeria?
A Baba Bomboy.

>>>>> **I'm a Frankfurter. What Are You?** <<<<<

A native of Sydney is a Sydneysider. People from Phoenix are Phoenixers. Praguers come from Prague and Edinburgers come from Edinburgh.

Then there are San Franciscans, San Diegans, San Antonians, St. Louisans, Melburnians, Honolulans, Houstonians, and Baltimoreans.

Then there are the names that sound just plain silly:

- Frankfurters (ketchup or mustard with that?) from Frankfurt

- Brummies from Birmingham

- Bolognese (getting hungry) from Bologna

- Cardiffians (sounds like a well-dressed pop band) from Cardiff

- Fort Wayniacs (metal band?) from Fort Wayne

- Glaswegians (half full or half empty) from Glasgow

- Las Vegans from Las Vegas (it's more of a carnivore's town . . .)

- Minneapolitans (new ice cream flavor?) from Minneapolis

- Parmesans (getting hungry again) from Parma

And let's not forget the Liverpudlians, Strasbourgeois, and Salemanders, respectively from Liverpool, Strasbourg, and Salem.

Potentially the worst names ever? Yats and Sluffs.

The former hail from New Orleans and sound like buzzing insects that come out at dusk. The latter hail from Slough in England and sound vaguely contagious.

Q What are the only five countries in the world with single-syllable names?

A Chad, France, Greece, Laos, and Spain. And no, Wales does not count—it's not a country (yet!).

Q What's the largest country in the world?

A Russia.

Q What country covers the most time zones?

A France if you include overseas territories, or Russia if you include only contiguous time zones.

Q What country has the highest incidence of depression?

A France. *Le boo hoo.*

Q What country is covered by more than 99 percent desert?

A Libya.

Q What is the country with the most languages spoken?

A Papua New Guinea, with more than 820 languages.

Q Name the only country with a double-triangle flag (instead of square or rectangular).

A Nepal.

1	New York City	A	Numidia
2	Istanbul	B	Formosa
3	Thailand	C	Persia
4	Sri Lanka	D	Ceylon
5	Myanmar	E	Burma
6	Cambodia	F	Kampuchea
7	Beijing	G	Peking
8	Democratic Republic of Congo	H	New Amsterdam
		I	Constantinople
9	Iran	J	Siam
10	Taiwan	K	British Honduras
11	Algeria	L	Zaire
12	Belize		

ANSWERS

1H, 2I, 3J, 4D, 5E, 6F, 7G, 8L, 9C, 10B, 11A, 12K

Q What country smokes the most marijuana each year on a per-capita basis?

A New Zealand.

Q Fourteen of the world's fifteen most unhappy countries are located where?

A Eastern Europe.

Q What is the world's most unhappy country?

A Bulgaria.

Q What country is least proud of its nationality?

A Japan.

Q What country comes in second place for least proud?

A Germany.

Q What three countries top the list for per-capita alcohol consumption?

A Luxcmbourg, France, and Ireland.

Q What country consumes the most bottled water?

A Italy.

Q What country eats the most pork per capita?

A Denmark.

Match the following countries to the lyrics of their national anthems:

1 Italy

2 Hungary

3 Burkina Faso

4 Algeria

5 Vietnam

6 France

7 Spain

A "When we spoke, none listened to us, so we have taken the noise of gunpowder as our rhythm, and the sound of machine guns as our melody."

B "The path to glory is built by the bodies of our foes!"

C "The Austrian eagle has already lost its plumes. The blood of Italy and the Polish blood it drank, along with the Cossack. But it burned its heart."

D "Anger gathered in your bosom and you struck with your lightning from your thundering clouds. Now the plundering Mongols' arrows."

E "Against the humiliating bondage of a thousand years, rapacity came from afar to subjugate them for a hundred years. Against the cynical malice in the shape of neo-colonialism and its petty local servants."

F This national anthem has no words.

G "Do you hear, in the countryside, the roar of those ferocious soldiers? They're coming right into your arms, to cut the throats of your sons and women!"

ANSWERS

1C, 2D, 3E, 4A, 5B, 6G, 7F.
Who knew national anthems were so brutal?! Hats off to the Spanish for having a wordless national anthem.

Q Name the only three countries in the world where more than half of the adult population smokes cigarettes?

A Nauru, Guinea, and Namibia.

Q What's the most heavily taxed nation on earth?

A Belgium, where the percentage of gross earnings given up in taxes exceeds 55 percent.

Q China consumes what percent of the world's annual rice crop?

A Approximately 34 percent.

Q What country exports the most bananas each year?

A India.

Q What country imports the most bananas each year?

A United States.

Q What country produces the most horsemeat for human consumption?

A Mexico.

Q In what country do one in five people believe the world will end in their lifetime?

A United States.

Q What three countries have the most roller coasters?

A United States, Japan, and United Kingdom, in that order.

➤ UNESCO'S WORLD HERITAGE LIST HONORS IRREPLACEABLE CULTURAL AND NATURAL HERITAGE SITES IN MORE THAN 160 COUNTRIES. WHICH COUNTRY BELOW DOES NOT HAVE ANY UNESCO WORLD HERITAGE SITES REGISTERED WITHIN ITS BORDERS?

A Jamaica

B Serbia

C Senegal

D Haiti

E Guatemala

ANSWER
　　Remarkably, the birthplace of Bob Marley has yet to list a site worthy of UNESCO preservation. That's not very *irie, mohn*.

Micronations:
Top Five Fake Countries

First off, let's be clear what micronations are *not*.

Micronations are not microstates such as Liechtenstein, San Marino, the Vatican, or Monaco—all of which are internationally recognized. Micronations are also not unrecognized states such as the Republic of China (aka Taiwan), the State of Palestine, or the Turkish Republic of Northern Cyprus—all of which operate as legitimate political entities but are not internationally recognized.

So what is a micronation? It is always small and a bit whacky. Micronations may be governed by self-proclaimed kings or queens, artists, political exiles, or mutants from outer space. All you really need is the courage to stand up and proclaim, "*This* land is *my* land."

1   Celestia. This micronation was founded in 1949 by James Thomas Mangan, Celestia's prime minister. Based in Evergreen Park, Illinois, Celestia is the earthly outpost for an empire that claims all known space in the sky as its sovereign territory. According to the prime minister, "We all travel through the sky 1,500,000 miles each day; and we are basically sky people—not earth people." Citizens of Celestia transact the nation's business using one of two gold-plated coins, the Joule and the Celeston, both featuring

portraits of Princess Ruth Marie Mangan, illustrious daughter of the prime minister. The status of the nation has been unclear since the death of Prime Minister Mangan in 1970.

2   Kingdom of Talossa. Talossans speak their own language, called *el glheþ Talossan*, and draft legislation through a *ziu* (parliament) overseen by benevolent King John. Talossa is a constitutional monarchy based in Milwaukee, Wisconsin, with an official population of 221. The kingdom was founded in 1979 by Robert Ben Madison, age 14. According to the nation's website, "The nation's founder, Robert Ben Madison, declared his second-floor bedroom to be an independent, sovereign country."

3   Kingdom of Lovely. The runner-up name for this country was "Kingdom of Home," which explains a lot. The country was founded in 2005 by Danny Wallace. He was the host of the BBC's documentary "How to Start Your Own Country." Wallace took his topic seriously and founded a country in the living room of his flat in East London. More than fifty-eight thousand people have registered online to become citizens of the Kingdom of Lovely. Wallace gained a fair bit of notoriety when he attempted to enter the 2006 Eurovision Song Contest with his heartfelt anthem, "Stop the Muggin', Start the Huggin'." His Eurovision application was denied.

4 State of Sabotage. This state has no defined territory. According to its founders—Robert Jelinek, H.R. Giger, and a 25-man screaming choir from Finland—the state may emerge anywhere, geographically. SoS is an art movement, music label, performance-art group, and secular-political collective that provokes thinking by intervening in the official discourse. "Sabotage is the experiment to break up incrustation of an organized bourgeois society that insulates itself against all changes and tries to make thinkable new possibilities." Since its founding on an uninhabited island in Finland in 2003, more than twelve thousand people have become SoS citizens.

5 Principality of Sealand. Often called the world's smallest nation, Sealand occupies a World War II naval fort located off England's southeast coast. It's been occupied since 1967 by Paddy Roy Bates and his family and friends; Bates took the fort from a band of pirate radio broadcasters and later declared it an independent nation. Interestingly, an English court declared in 1968 that Sealand is outside of Britain's territorial waters and not under British jurisdiction. Since then, more than 150,000 Sealand passports have been issued, despite the fact that no country officially recognizes Sealand.

ANIMAL KINGDOM

Animal Kingdom

TRUE OR FALSE? A group of apes is called a shrewdness.

TRUE.

TRUE OR FALSE? A whale's penis is called a dork.

FALSE.

It's just a penis. Don't trust everything you read on the Internet!

TRUE OR FALSE? A group of alligators is called a congregation.

TRUE.

Amen.

TRUE OR FALSE? The penis of most marsupials can split into two.

TRUE.

It's so that the penis can fit into the two vaginas common on female marsupials. What—you didn't know that female marsupials have two vaginas?

TRUE OR FALSE? A group of bears is called a sleuth.

TRUE.

Just like Sherlock Holmes. Nobody knows why.

TRUE OR FALSE? The blue whale has the largest penis of any organism on earth.

TRUE.

It can measure 8 to 10 feet long.

TRUE OR FALSE? A group of adult cats is called a pounce.

TRUE.

It's distinguished from a kindle, which is a group of kittens. Ahhhh.

TRUE OR FALSE? The female barkfly has a penis, which is used to extract sperm from the male barkfly's vagina.

TRUE.

And copulation among barkflies can last up to seventy hours!

TRUE OR FALSE? A group of cockroaches is called an intrusion.

TRUE.

On multiple levels.

TRUE OR FALSE? Female spotted hyenas have penises.

FALSE.

What looks like a penis on the female hyena is actually an engorged clitoris that measures up to 7 inches long.

TRUE OR FALSE? A group of doves is called a piteousness.

TRUE.

Maybe you've wondered why puppies, kittens, and babies are universally so cute and adorable.

Turns out it's not them. It's you.

Cuteness is one way that evolution encourages parents to look after their offspring. This is an especially important trait for mammalian parents. Insects, reptiles, and fish are born in vast numbers with no expectation that either parent will pay any attention to their offspring. Mammals, on the other hand, are typically dependent on one or both parents for months after birth. And this is evolution's cue to take life-or-death dependency and turn it into *ooohhh*-and-*aahhhhh* cuteness. It's like saying, "Mom, I'm so darn cute you just can't eat me or leave me."

The markers of "cuteness" in human babies include large eyes, small noses, and large cheeks and heads (in comparison to their bodies). Overwhelming cuteness transfers to the young of other mammals as well: dogs, cats, bears, mice, you name it.

TRUE OR FALSE? The penises of goats, kangaroos, yaks, donkeys, goats, bulls, and dogs are commonly eaten around the world.

TRUE.

TRUE OR FALSE? A group of hippopotamuses is called a bloat.

TRUE.

TRUE OR FALSE? Boars can ejaculate continuously for up to seven minutes.

TRUE.

And tiring.

TRUE OR FALSE? A group of owls is called a parliament.

TRUE.

TRUE OR FALSE? Some species of slugs have disposable penises that can be discarded after sex.

TRUE.

Stranger still, *Chromodoris reticulate* sea slugs are what is known as "simultaneous hermaphrodites," which means each individual has both a penis and a vagina—which it uses simultaneously during sex. And then . . . their penises fall off.

TRUE OR FALSE? A group of otters is called a romp.

TRUE.

TRUE OR FALSE? The penis of the Argentine bluebird duck is corkscrew-shaped and measures up to 17 inches long.

TRUE.

And consider this—the average height of the Argentine bluebird duck is only 16 inches.

1	Crows	A	Rabble
2	Buzzards	B	Wake
3	Foxes	C	Skulk
4	Gnats	D	Nest
5	Hyenas	E	Murder
6	Jellyfish	F	Plague
7	Mosquitoes	G	Unkindness
8	Ravens	H	Cackle
9	Vipers	I	Smack
10	Locusts	J	Scourge

ANSWERS

1E, 2B, 3C, 4A, 5H, 6I, 7J, 8G, 9D, 10F

TRUE OR FALSE? A group of flamingos is called a scurry.

FALSE.

A scurry is a group of squirrels.

TRUE OR FALSE? Male orb spiders remove their penises and insert them inside female orb spiders.

TRUE.

And you would too, if 75 percent of the time you were eaten by a hungry female orb spider during copulation.

TRUE OR FALSE? A pregnant goldfish is called a twat.

FALSE.

That's merely a legend.

TRUE OR FALSE? A severed cockroach head can survive for hours.

TRUE.

A severed cockroach head will survive for days if you keep it in the refrigerator.

TRUE OR FALSE? A decapitated cockroach can live for weeks before it starves to death.

TRUE.

A decapitated cockroach does not bleed to death, because its neck seals off the wound by clotting. A decapitated cockroach does not suffocate, since the cockroach brain controls neither breathing (cockroaches breathe through tiny holes all over their body) nor blood flow. And because cockroaches can survive for weeks on just one meal, zombie cockroaches that can live for weeks are totally real and totally in your house right now.

Did you know?

In 2012, a Florida man died after winning a cockroach-eating contest at a reptile store. It wasn't the cockroach that killed him; they are edible and frequently consumed in some cultures.

Instead, the likely cause of death was a rare allergic reaction to cockroach dandruff.

TRUE OR FALSE? Fleas can jump up to fifteen times their body length.

FALSE.

It's actually 150 times their body length, not fifteen. That's the equivalent of a human jumping more than 800 feet!

TRUE OR FALSE? Fleas can survive for up to one hundred days without a meal (e.g., without sucking your blood).

TRUE.

Unfortunately.

TRUE OR FALSE? When a flea emerges from its cocoon, it can jump more than four thousand times without food in search of its first meal.

TRUE.

And you just *knew* it had to be true, right?! Yuck.

TRUE OR FALSE? Fleas can be trained to perform in circuses.

FALSE.

Flea circuses are real, but fleas only live a few months and are not trained. Instead, performing fleas are permanently wired up or harnessed to props. Because fleas are strong they can pull much larger objects. The overall effect is that fleas can take directions and perform on cue, when they definitely cannot. The deeper philosophical question lurking here is: Who's the weirdo who first wired up a half-dozen fleas and staged them as a circus act?

TRUE OR FALSE? Cats are more popular pets than dogs.

TRUE.

At least in the United States. Domestic cats outnumber dogs by a few million. The difference is that most cat owners own more than one cat, so there are actually fewer cat-owning households in the U.S.

Did you know?

The first flea performances date from the sixteenth century, when watchmakers would demonstrate their mechanical skills by wiring fleas together. Circuses with actual fleas persisted in the United States and England up until the 1960s.

TRUE OR FALSE? If you own a cat, it's likely that your cat is fat or obese.

TRUE.

More than 50 percent of domestic cats are overweight. Indoor cats need just 180 calories per day (about twice that many calories come in a single serving of typical cat foods).

TRUE OR FALSE? People who spend a lot of time around cats are more likely to be neurotic.

TRUE.

But not for the reasons you may think. Cat feces contain a parasite called *Toxoplasma gondii*. The parasite has been shown to disrupt neurons in rats and mice, making them act in ways that make them more likely to be preyed upon by cats (the parasite only reproduces in cats). Recent studies suggest the effect is similar in humans too. In fact, up to a third of the global population of humans may already be infected. (Note to self: Don't eat cat feces.)

Cat or Dog?

Q

Domestic cats or household dogs, which species . . .

1 is more vocal?

2 is considered smarter by scientists?

3 is easier to house train?

4 has more teeth?

5 has a better memory?

6 has a better sense of smell?

7 sweats exclusively through their paws?

8 can detect an epileptic seizure in humans up to an hour before the seizure occurs?

9 should never eat chocolate?

10 prefers women to men?

11 spends 70 percent of its time sleeping and 30 percent of its awake time grooming?

1 Cat. Your average cat uses up to one hundred different vocalizations. Dogs, on the other hand, use a mere ten.

2 Dog. Multiple studies have shown dogs are more emotionally intelligent than cats; dogs are also more trainable, have larger brains, and are far more social (which promotes intelligence). Sorry, cat people. If it makes you feel better, other studies have shown that cat owners are smarter than people who own dogs.

3 Cat. They can be trained in a matter of minutes simply by placing a litter box in the house. No actual training is required—it's instinct that drives cats to use litter boxes.

4 Dog. Forty-two teeth for the average canine, compared to thirty teeth for domestic cats.

5 Cat. Dog memory is more "associative" instead of true memory. And dog short-term memory lasts for about twenty seconds.

6 Dog. The canine nose has more than four times as many scent receptors as the average cat nose (and more than fourteen times as many as the human nose).

7 Trick question: cat and dog. In both species, sweat glands are present only in the paws. To cool down, dogs pant. The thin ears of cats expose blood to ambient temperatures and help them to lose excess body heat.

8 Dog. So-called "seizure alert dogs" are able to detect changes in their owners' verbal cues and body language and warn them ahead of time. This skill is not taught—it's innate in a very small number of canines.

9 Another trick question: dog and cat. Most people know chocolate is toxic to dogs. Cats, too, can eat lethal doses of chocolate (or any food containing theobromine, which includes chocolate and tea). Cats cannot taste sweetness, however, so the odds are lower of cats gorging on your half-eaten chocolate bar.

10 The final trick question: cat and dog. Studies show that dogs respond with less aggression, and cats display positive reciprocation when interacting with women rather than men.

11 Cat. Duh!

TRUE OR FALSE? Cats can be left-handed.

TRUE.

Cats use both paws for simple tasks like swatting at a ball. But for complex tasks, female cats are almost universally right-pawed and male cats almost always favor their left paw. A very small percentage appear ambidextrous.

TRUE OR FALSE? Most cats have three eyelids.

TRUE.

A third eyelid promotes healthy eyes. In fact, having three eyelids is common for most mammals and birds. Humans are the odd species out, having just two eyelids (one upper, one lower) per eye.

TRUE OR FALSE? The mayor of Talkeetna, Alaska, is a cat.

TRUE.

His name is Stubbs (Mayor Stubbs to you!), and he has been mayor of the historical district of Talkeetna for more than fifteen years. He was a write-in candidate, originally.

TRUE OR FALSE? Each year nearly 4 million cats are eaten in China as a delicacy.

TRUE.

Cat meat sells for roughly 160 yuan ($26) per kilogram.

TRUE OR FALSE? Cat urine glows under a black light.

TRUE.

Like most mammal urine, cat pee contains large amounts of phosphorous, which glows under ultraviolet light.

TRUE OR FALSE? Cow's milk gives most cats a case of diarrhea.

TRUE.

Cats are generally lactose intolerant when it comes to cow's milk. Think twice before refilling that saucer of milk next to the litter box.

TRUE OR FALSE? Most birds poop, lay eggs, and mate using the very same body part.

TRUE.

It's a multifaceted hole called a "cloaca." Birds have sex by putting their cloacas together, and females lay eggs from it. It's also where waste is excreted.

TRUE OR FALSE? Birds do not pee.

TRUE.

Bird poop is white because birds do not urinate. Instead, their kidneys produce uric acid that is excreted as a white paste.

TRUE OR FALSE? It's healthy for animals to eat their own poop.

MOSTLY TRUE.

Some animals eat their own poop because it contains nutrients that are produced by intestinal bacteria. Other animals have high-fiber diets that are difficult to fully absorb on the first pass through the digestive system. Animals that eat poop on a regular basis (both their own and the poop of others) include rabbits, gorillas, dung beetles, houseflies, and dogs.

TRUE OR FALSE? Dogs generally prefer to eat the protein-rich poop of cats.

TRUE.

Think about that the next time your dog gives you a big sloppy tongue kiss!

TRUE OR FALSE? Humans are the only animals that keep pet dogs.

FALSE.

Troops of African baboons have been known to capture and raise young feral dogs. Apparently the baboons crave companionship and protection from the wild canines—just like us humans.

TRUE OR FALSE? Not all dogs bark.

TRUE.

The Basenji breed from central Africa is physically incapable of barking. What sound does it make? It yodels, of course.

TRUE OR FALSE? The sound a kangaroo makes is known as a bark.

FALSE.

Kangaroos actually chortle.

TRUE OR FALSE? Mice, narwhals, orangutans, and bonobos are all capable of squealing.

TRUE.

Pigs squeal too.

TRUE OR FALSE? Piranhas grunt.

TRUE.

The red-bellied piranha (one of the species that *will* eat humans) grunts aggressively to ward off other piranhas.

TRUE OR FALSE? Some fish can walk.

TRUE.

The mudskipper lives completely in the water and yet is able to walk on land, on its fins.

TRUE OR FALSE? Some fish can do flips and jump up to 2 feet in the air.

TRUE.

All hail the mighty mudskipper!

The plural of "fish" is "fish."

It's true. Strict grammarians use "fishes" only when referring to multiple species of fish.

TRUE OR FALSE? Flying fish have been clocked gliding above the water at more than 40 miles per hour.

TRUE.

They can also achieve an altitude of 20 feet and cover more than 1,300 feet in a single glide.

TRUE OR FALSE? Some fish can live out of water for weeks on end.

PARTLY TRUE.

The African lungfish can actually live for *months,* not weeks, breathing air. It's one of the few fish with both gills and a lung.

TRUE OR FALSE? Catfish have a better sense of taste than humans.

TRUE.

We're not talking about fashion or art, but about flavor. Humans have an average of ten thousand taste buds on their tongues. Channel catfish, by contrast, have upwards of 100,000 taste buds distributed all over their body. It makes sense when you realize that catfish spend their days swimming in dark, murky water.

TRUE OR FALSE? Fish cannot swim backward.

MOSTLY TRUE.

Only some species of eel and lamprey can actually swim backward. All other fish swim forward only.

TRUE OR FALSE? Electric eels generate enough electric charge to kill a horse—or a human.

TRUE.

And shocking.

TRUE OR FALSE? Hangfish can fill a gallon-size bucket with slime in less than one minute.

TRUE.

And completely gross. Their prodigious slime production makes them unappetizing prey.

TRUE OR FALSE? Many lipsticks contain fish scales.

TRUE.

It's what gives some lipsticks and nail polishes their shimmer and gleam.

TRUE OR FALSE? Fish, jellyfish, frogs, and toads have all been known to fall out of the sky.

TRUE.

It's a rare meteorological phenomenon typically caused by strong winds or tornadoes that lift hundreds of creatures out of rivers or shallow oceans and deposit them miles inland. Heads up.

TRUE OR FALSE? Squid have the largest eyes of any animal on Earth.

TRUE.

The giant Antarctic squid is the largest squid known, with an eye that's sixteen times wider than a human eye—roughly one foot in diameter!

TRUE OR FALSE? An ostrich's eye is larger than its brain.

TRUE.

Though don't call them stupid. Ostriches have really big eyes. So it's better to think of this as a "large eye" rather than a "small brain" sort of problem.

TRUE OR FALSE? Most species of octopus can fit through any opening larger than their beak.

TRUE.

The average octopus beak is 2 to 3 inches in diameter. Octopuses have neither bones nor rigid skeletons, so they are able to squeeze their entire bodies through incredibly small openings.

TRUE OR FALSE? The Cyclops is a one-eyed albino shark that swims in the waters off California.

FALSE.

But only just! A one-eyed albino fetus was found in the belly of an endangered dusky shark in 2011 off the California coast. The fetus suffered from a rare genetic disease and was not actually a new species of shark . . . much to the relief of surfers and seals everywhere.

TRUE OR FALSE? The following animals have been found in the stomachs of Greenland sharks: moose, polar bears, horses, and entire reindeer.

TRUE.

The Greenland shark is not to be messed with.

Butterflies taste with their antennae.

FALSE.

They actually taste with their feet, with sensors that detect whether the leaf underfoot is edible for their caterpillars (adult butterflies don't chew, they suck nectar).

The sting of a killer bee is deadly.

FALSE.

African honeybees, the so-called killer bees, are exactly like other honeybees when it comes to their physiology. Their sting is no more dangerous than that of other honeybees. What makes them more dangerous, though, is more aggressive behavior that can include clustering in groups and stinging intruders multiple times.

Scorpions were among the first animals to migrate from the sea to land.

TRUE.

Scorpion fossils date as far back as 420 million years. Apparently these were amphibious scorpions that measured more than 3 feet long. Yuck.

Scorpions are insects.

FALSE.

Scorpions are arachnids just like ticks, mites, and spiders.

Mammals don't eat arachnids.

FALSE.

Humans, meerkats, and many other mammals regularly eat arachnids, including scorpions.

Elephants are the only mammals that can't jump.

_____

FALSE.

   While it's true that elephants cannot jump, it's also true that rhinos, sloths, and hippos cannot jump.

Elephants are the only mammals with four knees.

_____

FALSE.

   There is no mammal with four knees. The joints in their forelimbs bend backward, and are equivalent to human wrist joints. Death to another popular Internet myth!

Naked mole rats can use their two long front teeth like chopsticks, spreading them apart and pushing them together.

_____

TRUE.

   They are one of the few mammals that can move their front teeth independently.

Giraffes sleep the least of any mammal.

_____

TRUE.

   Giraffes generally sleep for less than two hours a day, in increments of just five to ten minutes.

Sloths sleep the longest of any mammal.

_____

FALSE.

   The koala actually owns the title for longest sleeping mammal, at twenty-two hours per day.

TRUE OR FALSE? Some species don't sleep at all.

TRUE.

Some sharks, including hammerheads, as well as mackerels have the ability to skip sleep altogether. Among vertebrates, only fish can survive without sleep.

TRUE OR FALSE? Among mammals, walruses hold the record for staying awake the longest.

TRUE.

Walruses can swim continuously for more than eighty hours at a time. They do this frequently too.

TRUE OR FALSE? Cows and horses sleep with their eyes open.

TRUE, MOSTLY.

Cows and horses can sleep with closed eyes. They often sleep with open eyes and while standing up, however (both animals have the ability to lock their knees and stay standing even when asleep).

TRUE OR FALSE? Thirty-two pigeons, twenty-eight dogs, three horses, and one cat have received medals for bravery in wartime.

TRUE.

The PDSA Dickin Medal was established in 1943 to honor the work of animals in military service. The most recent recipient was a dog named Sasha, a bomb-sniffing Labrador retriever who died on duty in Afghanistan in 2008.

TRUE OR FALSE? The king of Norway knighted a penguin in 2008, proclaiming the creature "in every way qualified to receive the honor and dignity of knighthood."

TRUE.

Colonel-in-Chief Sir Nils Olav is a king penguin at Scotland's Edinburgh Zoo. Sir Olav (and his predecessors—also named Nils Olav) is the mascot of the Norwegian King's Guard. Sir Olav gets a promotion each time the King's Guard visits Edinburgh Zoo.

TRUE OR FALSE? The brontosaurus never existed.

TRUE.

The name means "thunder lizard," but scientifically speaking the brontosaurus is a fiction. What scientists in the late nineteenth century thought was a new species of dinosaur was actually an apatosaurus. Break the news gently to your dino-loving kids.

TRUE OR FALSE? More than a third of all previously identified dinosaur species never existed.

FALSE.

But close! Scientists estimate that many dinosaur fossils do not represent new species, but instead are juvenile specimens from established species. It's like finding fossils of a young deer lacking antlers and an adult deer with antlers, and assuming they are different species.

TRUE OR FALSE? 99.9 percent of all species that have existed on Earth are extinct.

TRUE.

Most species don't last millions of years. Your species is lucky to get a few hundred thousand years, to be honest.

TRUE OR FALSE? The worst mass extinction killed 95 percent of species on Earth.

TRUE.

It happened 251 million years ago and is called the Permian-Triassic extinction. Whether it was caused by a comet or asteroid, or perhaps volcanic activity, nobody is certain. What is clear is that most life on Earth disappeared in the relatively short span of a few million years.

TRUE OR FALSE? We are living through a sixth period of mass extinction on Earth.

TRUE.

We're losing species at a rate 100 times above historical averages. And unlike previous mass extinctions, this one is mostly due to human activity.

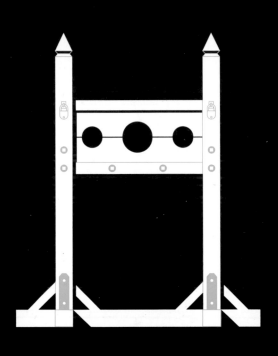

CRIME

PUNISHMENT

Crime & Punishment

Q Who was the world's first police detective?

A Eugène François Vidocq. The Frenchman founded the plainclothes civil police unit, the Brigade de la Sûreté, in 1812.

Q Who created the world's first detective agency?

A Eugène François Vidocq. In 1833 he founded the world's first private detective agency, known as Le bureau des renseignements. Vidocq pioneered the concept of undercover work and wore disguises and even faked his own death in pursuit of criminals. Vidocq is also credited with introducing the study of ballistics in criminology, and he was the first person to cast a shoe print in plaster for evidence.

Q Who was the world's first fictional police detective?

A C. Auguste Dupin. Edgar Allan Poe used Eugène François Vidocq as a model for his character C. Auguste Dupin in the 1841 short story "The Murders in the Rue Morgue," which is considered the world's first detective story.

Q What was the name of Britain's first detective branch?

A Scotland Yard. London's Metropolitan Police established a detective branch in 1842, headquartered in a building that backed onto a courtyard named Great Scotland Yard. The name "Scotland Yard" stuck.

Q Members of London's Metropolitan Police Force are known by what nickname?

A Bobbies. The nickname is an ode to their founder, Sir Robert Peal, who established the force in 1829. Contrary to popular belief, the nickname "coppers" or "cop" for the police likely comes from the Latin *capere*, to seize, and is probably not a reference to the copper buttons or badges worn by nineteenth-century British police.

 **Did you know?**

A real-life member of Scotland Yard, Inspector Charles Frederick Field, was friends with author Charles Dickens and introduced Dickens to London's criminal haunts. Dickens later featured the inspector in his 1851 short story "On Duty with Inspector Field."

Q What illicit substances does Sherlock Holmes habitually use in Arthur Conan Doyle's stories?

A Cocaine, heroin, and morphine.

Q Who were Sheridan Hope and Ormond Sacker?

A The original names for Arthur Conan Doyle's infamous crime-solving duo, Sherlock Holmes and Dr. John Watson. Hope and Sacker first appeared in a novel called *A Tangled Skein*. Besides a change in the lead characters' names, Doyle changed the novel's title to *A Study in Scarlet* when it was officially published in 1887.

Q In Arthur Conan Doyle's stories, how many times does Sherlock Holmes utter the phrase, "Elementary, my dear Watson"?

A Zero. The phrase does not appear in any of the sixty Sherlock Holmes stories written by Sir Arthur Conan Doyle. Holmes often says "elementary" and "My dear Watson," but never together.

Q When Sherlock Holmes retired from solving crimes, what did he become?

A A beekeeper.

Q Is the nineteenth-century serial killer Jack the Ripper real or fictional?

A Real, though with a caveat. The name "Jack the Ripper" is the name given to an unidentified serial killer who terrorized London in the 1880s and '90s. The killer targeted prostitutes, slitting their throats and mutilating their bodies. At least five murders have been pinned on Jack the Ripper, with some estimating as many as sixteen or seventeen total victims.

Did you know?

Sir Arthur Conan Doyle has sold more books than
J.K. Rowling and J.R.R. Tolkien combined!

➤ **WHICH OF THE FOLLOWING SERIAL-KILLER NICKNAMES
IS FAKE?**

A Zodiac Killer

B Dating Game Killer

C Eyeball Killer

D Angel of Death

E Son of Sam

F Gorilla Man

G Hillside Strangler

H Gummy Bear Killer

I Shoe Fetish Slayer

J Jolly Black Widow

K Werewolf of Wisteria

L The Killer Clown

M The Happy Face Killer

ANSWER H.
Happily, nobody has yet defamed gummy bears in the pursuit of serial-
killer fame.

Q Which of the above serial killers is the only one never caught,
captured, or identified?

A The Zodiac Killer. He was active in California in the 1960s,
killing at least seven people and taunting police with coded
letters and cryptic puzzles that are still unsolved. The case
remains open.

Q Cult leader Charles Manson took his inspiration for a global race war from which Beatles' song?

A "Helter Skelter." Manson and his followers, called The Family, murdered seven people, including the actress Sharon Tate. Manson was convicted of murder and is locked up today in California's Corcoran State Prison.

Q What was the name of the album Charles Manson released in 1970 to help pay for his legal defense during his murder trial?

A *Lie: The Love and Terror Cult.*

Q What band infamously covered a Charles Manson song on a 1993 album?

A Guns N' Roses. Their cover of Manson's song "Look at Your Game, Girl" appeared on their 1993 album *The Spaghetti Incident?*

Q Who is the deadliest serial killer in modern times?

A Colombia's Luis Garavito. He killed at least 140 children during the 1990s.

Q Who are the deadliest serial killers in the United States?

A Henry Lee Lucas (confessed to 350 victims, though only eleven were proven), Gary Ridgway (seventy-one confessed victims), Ted Bundy (thirty-six confessed victims), John Wayne Gacy (thirty-three confessed victims,) and Jeffrey Dahmer (seventeen victims).

Q What did serial killer John Wayne Gacy dress up as when hunting for his victims?

A A clown. Gacy met his victims, typically teenage boys, wearing a homemade clown costume. He introduced himself as "Pogo the Clown."

Q What made serial killer Jeffrey Dahmer especially notorious?

A Police discovered that Jeffrey Dahmer would drill into the skulls of his victims and have sex with them, while they were still alive. He also ate some of his victims. The good news? Dahmer was eventually beaten to death by an inmate in jail.

Q What made killer Ed Gein especially notorious?

A Ed Gein confessed to only two murders, but his penchant for the macabre made him an inspiration for the Alfred Hitchcock movie *Psycho*. When Ed Gein's mother and brother died, he began digging up bodies at cemeteries looking for women who resembled his mother. After he was arrested, police discovered skulls made into bowls, chairs upholstered in human flesh, and a belt made out of female nipples.

Q What reason did serial killer Edmund Kemper give for killing his grandparents at age 15?

A He "just wanted to see what it felt like to kill Grandma." Edmund Kemper was active in California in the 1970s. He killed six women as well as his mother and grandparents.

➤ **WHICH OF THE FOLLOWING ARE NOT ACTUAL WEAPONS IN THE BOARD GAME CLUE (OR CLUEDO IF YOU GREW UP IN THE U.K.)?**

A Candlestick

B Knife

C Wrench

D Lead pipe

E Hatchet

F Revolver

G Rope

H Ice pick

ANSWER

Hatchet and ice pick. All the other weapons are from the game.

Q If you plan to poison somebody with hemlock, how much will you need?

A At least six petals of hemlock's toxic flower. The seeds and roots are also deadly. The Greek philosopher Socrates was sentenced to death by drinking a chalice of poison derived from hemlock.

Q How are Napoleon Bonaparte, Britain's King George III, and Simón Bolívar thought to have died?

A From an overdose of the poison arsenic.

Cruel and Very Unusual

In ancient and medieval times, the following forms of capital punishment were commonly used to rid the world of murderers, rapists, and traitors.

- The wheel: Lashed to a wagon wheel and your limbs bludgeoned or broken by brute force.

- Boiled: Immersed in a cauldron of boiling water, oil, or tar; alternatively, immersed in a shallow container of liquid and fried to death.

- Flaying: The removal of a person's skin. Unfortunately for the victim, the cause of death can be anything from hypothermia to shock. Equally unfortunate, it can take a day or two to die once your skin has been removed.

- Death by a thousand cuts: This was a popular form of execution in China until the twentieth century. Victims were lashed to a frame and, over a period of days, pieces of their bodies were severed by a knife.

- Disembowelment: Cut an opening in a person's abdomen and start removing organs, particularly the bowels.

- Crucifixion: Tie or nail the victim to a cross, and leave them hanging until they die.

- Impalement: Driving a pointed stake through a victim's body, generally from the rectum up through the breast or shoulder.

- Crushing by elephant: Popular in southeast Asia from the eleventh to the eighteenth centuries. Tie up victim, place under elephant foot . . . and stand back.

- Stoning: Gather large group of people, distribute large quantity of stones, throw stones at victim. The point here is that no single person is responsible; it's a group act.

- Burning: Sometimes called burning at the stake or *auto-da-fé*. All methods involve exposing the victim to direct flames or heat.

- Decapitation: Removal of the victim's head by knife, sword, axe, or other blade. The guillotine is the poster child and most famous instrument of decapitation.

- Hanged, drawn, and quartered: Reserved specifically for traitors against English kings in the fourteenth to seventeenth centuries. Victims were dragged or drawn behind a horse to a platform where they were then hanged, removed just before the moment of death, and then castrated, disemboweled, beheaded, and quartered (all four limbs severed from the body).

TRUE OR FALSE? The act of hanging, drawing, and quartering was not abolished in England until 1870.

TRUE.

TRUE OR FALSE? Stoning remains legal today in Iran, Qatar, Saudi Arabia, Somalia, Sudan, Yemen, and Pakistan.

TRUE.

TRUE OR FALSE? The 1699 Shoplifting Act in England made it a capital crime to steal items worth more than 5 shillings (about $50 today).

TRUE.

In lieu of death, convicted shoplifters could also choose to be "transported" and permanently exiled to North America or Australia. Cheers, mate.

TRUE OR FALSE? First-degree murder, sabotage, train wrecking causing death, treason, and perjury causing execution of an innocent person are all capital crimes in the state of California.

TRUE.

So, too, is fatal assault by a prisoner serving a life sentence!

TRUE OR FALSE? Alabama was the first U.S. state to use lethal injection as a form of capital punishment.

FALSE.

That ignominious distinction belongs to Texas, which used lethal injection for the first time in 1982.

TRUE OR FALSE? The countries with the most state-sanctioned executions are China, Iran, Iraq, Saudi Arabia, and the United States.

TRUE.

TRUE OR FALSE? Despite the fact that the United Nations, the Geneva Convention, and American law outlaw torture, the U.S. government sanctioned the use of water boarding during the Afghanistan war.

TRUE.

Water boarding is an interrogation technique that simulates drowning. A victim is strapped to a board, face up and head down, while water is poured continuously into their mouth and nose. The CIA has since destroyed at least ninety-two videos of suspected terrorist interrogations using techniques such as water boarding.

TRUE OR FALSE? One in four convicts ultimately exonerated by DNA evidence confessed or pled guilty to crimes they did not commit.

TRUE.

TRUE OR FALSE? You can be sent to jail for one year in Singapore if your suicide attempt fails.

TRUE.

Singapore is one of the many countries that criminalize suicide.

⟫⟫⟫⟫⟫ Four Tips to Avoid False Confessions ⟪⟪⟪⟪⟪

The next time you are being interrogated by police, watch out for these four common techniques used to extract a confession from you!

1 *Direct confrontation:* Suggesting they know you committed the crime. If they say, "I know you did it, just admit it," you can be sure they don't know you did it.

2 *Theme development:* Offering you an excuse or rationalization for what you did. When they say, "The world is a harsh place; I understand why you would do that," don't believe it.

3 *Dealing with resistance:* Whey they talk over you, confront you, or get you to talk when you're trying not to, your resistance is being dealt with.

4 *Alternative questioning:* When they ask you if you committed the crime because you needed the money, or just because you wanted to get your name in the papers, you're being presented with a false dilemma that could get you to spill the beans.

Cult leader Jim Jones inspired more than nine hundred followers to kill themselves in 1978 by drinking cyanide-laced punch.

TRUE.

Jim Jones is responsible for the largest mass suicide in American history. The leader and founder of the Peoples Temple, Jones fled the United States in 1974 and set up a compound in Guyana, South America, called Jonestown. After a U.S. congressman visited Jonestown in 1978, a handful of Peoples Temple disciples decided to flee and return to the United States. Jones ordered the assassination of the congressman and his entourage. Later on the same day, Jones incited 909 of his followers (including more than three hundred children) to drink cyanide-laced punch. Jones himself died from a self-inflicted gunshot wound to the head.

TRUE OR FALSE? The largest bank robbery in history netted the robbers more than $1 billion worth of $100 bills.

TRUE.

Qusay Hussein, one of Saddam Hussein's sons, carried a note from his father authorizing the massive withdrawal from Iraq's Central Bank in 2005, just hours before the country was invaded. Qusay was eventually killed by U.S. forces, who recovered $650 million of the stolen money. The remaining $350 million was never found.

TRUE OR FALSE? The loot from the second-largest bank robbery in history weighed more than 7,000 pounds.

TRUE.

It happened in 2005 in Brazil. Robbers dug a 656-foot tunnel underneath the Banco Central in the city of Fortaleza and made off with more than $69 million worth of Brazilian reals. Authorities estimate that the stolen cash weighed more than 7,000 pounds. Only some of the cash has been recovered.

TRUE OR FALSE? According to the Federal Bureau of Investigation, the average haul for a bank robbery in the United States is $4,029.

TRUE.

If you work with a partner, divide that number by two. The average haul for a pickpocket is $504. Shoplifters earn a why-even-bother $181 per theft.

TRUE OR FALSE? The largest theft so far in the twenty-first century happened in the very same hotel where the movie *To Catch a Thief* was filmed.

TRUE.

In 2013, an unknown thief stole $136 million worth of jewels from an Israeli billionaire who was staying at the Intercontinental Hotel in Cannes, France. By coincidence or not, the hotel was featured in the 1955 heist film.

TRUE OR FALSE? Airline hijacker D.B. Cooper jumped from a plane above rural Washington state—and has never been seen since.

TRUE.

In 1971, D.B. Cooper hijacked a plane traveling between Portland, Oregon, and Seattle, Washington. Cooper demanded $200,000 in ransom money and four parachutes, which he received after the plane temporarily landed in Seattle. Cooper forced the crew to take off again heading for Mexico, and he demanded that the cabin remain unpressurized. At some point near Mount Saint Helens, Cooper jumped from the plane, in the dark, in the rain, wearing a trench coat. It's the last anybody has ever seen of him.

The prison on Alcatraz Island is escape proof.

UNCLEAR.

Alcatraz was deemed "escape proof" when it opened as a federal prison in 1934. Twelve unsuccessful escape attempts were made, all ending in the recapture of the inmates. Two escape attempts were possibly successful, however. In 1937, Theodore Cole and Ralph Roe filed through the bars and fled into the cold and swift-moving waters of San Francisco Bay; the two men are presumed drowned. In 1962, Frank Morris and the brothers John and Clarence Anglin escaped using an elaborate plan that included dummies left behind in their beds and building a makeshift raft from raincoats. The men were never found and the case remains open.

TRUE OR FALSE? Real estate mogul Leona Helmsley left $12 million in her will to a dog named Trouble.

TRUE.

At the time of her death in 2007, Leona Helmsley was worth a reported $2.5 billion. In her will she left $12 million to her dog, a Maltese named Trouble.

TRUE OR FALSE? The largest tax fraud in U.S. history involved more than $7 billion in fraudulent tax deductions.

TRUE.

Chicago lawyer Paul Daugerdas was convicted in 2012 of generating more than $7 billion in fraudulent tax deductions and more than $1 billion in phony losses for his wealthy clients. The Internal Revenue Service was not impressed.

>>>>>>>>>>> **Five Great Heist Films** <<<<<<<<<<<

1 Steven Soderbergh's *Ocean's Eleven* is a 2002 classic about taking down a Las Vegas casino. Having Brad Pitt and George Clooney in the cast doesn't hurt, either. It's a remake of sorts of the 1960 film of the same name starring Frank Sinatra, Dean Martin, Sammy Davis Jr., Peter Lawford, and Angie Dickinson.

2 *The Killing* is Stanley Kubrick's first brush with fame. It's about a crook who takes on the storied "one last job." Never a smart idea.

3 *Point Break* is a 1991 classic directed by Kathryn Bigelow and starring Patrick Swayze, Keanu Reeves, and Gary Busey. Surfers, bank robbers sporting masks of U.S. presidents, and a mildly spaced-out Keanu Reeves make this a must-see.

4 *Bonnie and Clyde* is the 1967 classic starring Warren Beatty and Faye Dunaway. Best line from the movie? "This here's Miss Bonnie Parker. I'm Clyde Barrow. We rob banks."

5 The 1975 Oscar-winning *Dog Day Afternoon* stars Al Pacino and John Cazale. It's a true story about a sad-sack man who robs a bank to pay for his boyfriend's sex-change operation. Mainly it's a lesson in how not to rob a bank.

TRUE OR FALSE? Lawyers must meet moral-character criteria that include honesty, fairness, candor, and trustworthiness.

TRUE.

TRUE OR FALSE? Lawyers cannot disclose any information told to them by clients.

FALSE.
Lawyers have an obligation to disclose information if they believe their client intends to commit bodily harm.

Q Who said, "As things got heated, I just remember Nicole fell and hurt herself. And this guy kind of got into a karate thing . . . I remember I grabbed the knife."

A O.J. Simpson

Q Gregory Liascos of Oregon attempted to tunnel into a museum of rocks and minerals disguised as what?

A A shrub. He wore a moss- and leaf-covered camouflage suit hoping the museum guards would not notice him. The police dog was not fooled.

Q The Federal Bureau of Investigation arrested Jules Bahr after he posted a photo of what on his Facebook page?

A The machine gun he used to rob a bank earlier in the day.

Q What sign did a judge order two convicted shoplifters to hold outside of a Wal-Mart in Alabama?

A A sign reading, "I am a thief, I stole from Wal-Mart."

Q Is it illegal to wrestle a bear in Alabama?

A Yes. It's a Class B felony.

Q Until what year was it a valid defense against rape or sexual battery in Mississippi to claim that the female victim was not chaste in character?

A Until 1998.

Q In London, is it illegal for a person with the plague to flag down a taxi or ride on a bus?

A Yes. The Public Health Act of 1984 makes it a crime. Ditto if you have leprosy or rabies.

Q Is it legal for women in Greece to wear stiletto heels at ancient archaeological sites?

A No, it is illegal. The heels apparently can leave permanent marks.

Q Is it illegal to share a hotel room in the United Arab Emirates with someone of the opposite sex to whom you are not married or closely related?

A Yes.

1 Lindsay Lohan vs. E*TRADE. The claim? E*TRADE's 2010 Super Bowl ad featured a talking baby named "Lindsay," portrayed as a milkaholic. Allegedly this ad was subliminally about Lindsay Lohan. And Lindsay wanted $100 million to make the pain go away.

2 Allan Heckard vs. Michael Jordan. The claim? Michael Jordan allegedly looks like him, wears an earring like him, and has a shaved head like him, causing people everywhere to approach him and ask for autographs. So in 2006, Heckard sued Michael Jordan and Nike founder Phil Knight for $832 million in Oregon state court. Never mind that Heckard was 6 inches shorter and 30 pounds heavier than Jordan.

3 Anna Ayala vs. the fast food chain Wendy's. The claim? She found a finger in her Wendy's chili. The reality? Anna planted the severed finger in her own chili and served four years in prison. She was paroled in 2010 under one condition: Never again set foot in a Wendy's.

4 Cleanthi Peters vs. Universal Studios. The claim? The haunted house at Universal's "Halloween Horror Nights" was too scary. Boo!

5 Richard Overton vs. Anheuser-Busch. The claim? False and misleading advertising. Apparently when Overton drank a bottle of Budweiser, scantily clad women in bikinis did not magically appear and invite him to play a game of beach volleyball.

6 Lauren Rosenberg vs. Patrick Harwood. The claim? Google Maps caused Lauren Rosenberg to walk on a freeway to reach her destination. Along the way she was hit by a car driven by Patrick Harwood. Both the driver and Google were sued for $100,000.

MUSIC

• CHAPTER 11 •

Music

TRUE OR FALSE? If you perform the lyrics of "Happy Birthday to You" for profit, you owe royalties to Warner/ Chappell Music, a division of the Warner Music Group.

TRUE.

It's estimated that the "Happy Birthday to You" song earns Warner Music up to $5,000 in royalties per day.

TRUE OR FALSE? Warner Music charges up to $10,000 to sing the "Happy Birthday to You" song in a public broadcast.

TRUE.

It's why you almost never hear the song performed on your favorite television show or film.

TRUE OR FALSE? The drummer on the Beatle's first single, *Love Me Do*, earned £5 for the session and no royalties.

TRUE.

Poor Andy White. That's right, Andy White. Who?! Most people have never heard of him.

TRUE OR FALSE? Before the Beatles became the Beatles, they were known the Beatals.

TRUE.

Before becoming the Beatles, the band was also known as the Blackjacks, the Quarrymen, Johnny and the Moondogs, the Beatals, the Silver Beetles, and the Silver Beatles.

TRUE OR FALSE? None of the Beatles could read music.

TRUE.

TRUE OR FALSE? Paul McCartney's real first name is Paul.

FALSE.

It's James.

TRUE OR FALSE? Pop star George Michael's real name is Georgios Panayiotou.

TRUE.

TRUE OR FALSE? The bass player and co-lead singer of the band Kiss is named Chaim Witz.

TRUE.

But you may know him better as Gene Simmons. He also goes by the names Dr. Love and The Demon.

TRUE OR FALSE? The real name of the Ramone's Tommy Ramone is Erdélyi Tamás.

TRUE.

He was born in Hungary.

TRUE OR FALSE? The real name of pop star Lorde is Ella Marija Lani Yelich-O'Connor.

TRUE.

TRUE OR FALSE? John Denver's real name was Henry John Deutschendorf Jr.

TRUE.

TRUE OR FALSE? Stevie Wonder was born as Steveland Judkins.

TRUE.

TRUE OR FALSE? Frank Sinatra's real name was Ricardo Valente Lopez.

FALSE.

It was just Francis Sinatra.

TRUE OR FALSE? Beyoncé tried to trademark the name of her daughter, Blue Ivy.

TRUE.

Beyoncé and Jay-Z filed a trademark application in 2012 to use their daughter's name for a branded line of diapers, "non-medicated hair care preparations," and "electric hair-curlers" among others. The patent office refused some uses—there's already a trademarked Blue Ivy wedding-planning company in Massachusetts—but left open the possibility to trademark the name in other categories.

1	Ringo Starr	A	Paul Hewson
2	Cher	B	Richard Starkey
3	Lady Gaga	C	Robert Allen Zimmerman
4	Jay-Z	D	Cherilyn Sarkisian
5	Katy Perry	E	Shawn Corey Carter
6	Bono	F	Katheryn Hudson
7	Elton John	G	Reginald Kenneth Dwight
8	Snoop Dog	H	Cordozar Calvin Broadus
9	Jack White	I	Stefani Joanne Angelina Germanotta
10	Bob Dylan	J	John Anthony Gillis
11	Eminem	K	Marshal Mathers

ANSWERS

1B, 2D, 3I, 4E, 5F, 6A, 7G, 8H, 9J, 10C, 11K

Q What did Elvis Presley never do during his entire career?

A Write a song. Elvis famously never wrote a song, nor had an idea for a song. He's what you'd call a performer in the truest sense.

Q What year did the first Elvis impersonator perform?

A 1956. Long before he died, Elvis had numerous impersonators performing his music and mimicking his style.

Q What did Elvis buy at a hardware store on his 11th birthday?

A His first guitar. It cost less than $8.

A He was a black belt in karate.

B He asked President Nixon to make him an FBI agent-at-large at a 1970 meeting at the White House.

C His first public performance was at the Mississippi-Alabama Fair and Dairy Show.

D Until his teens, he was blond.

E He had a pet chimpanzee.

F He was a descendant of Abraham Lincoln and distant cousin of President Jimmy Carter.

244

G He has sold more than 1 billion albums worldwide and has been awarded 110 gold, platinum, and multiplatinum singles and albums.

H He had a pet giraffe.

I He met his future wife, Priscilla Beaulieu, when she was 14 years old.

ANSWER

H. Elvis never had a pet giraffe. In case you're wondering, his pet chimpanzee was named Scatter.

Q What does the organization NAAEI do?

A The National Association of Amateur Elvis Impersonators (NAAEI) is a trade group for aspiring Elvis impresarios.

Q Who founded the NAAEI?

A Nude Elvis, aka David Woo-Bloxberg.

Q Whom has *Rolling Stone* magazine twice listed as the Number One greatest guitar player of all time?

A Jimi Hendrix. He earned top honors in lists published in 2003 and 2011.

Q Whom did guitar manufacturer Gibson list as the Number One guitar player of all time?

A Jimi Hendrix.

Q Whom did *Spin* magazine co-list as the Number One guitar players of all time?

A Lee Ranaldo and Thurston Moore from the band Sonic Youth. Hmmm.

Q What did Leo Fender, inventor of the Telecaster, Stratocaster, and Precision Bass guitars, not know how to play?

A The guitar.

Q What educational degree does Brian May, lead guitarist for the band Queen, have?

A PhD in astrophysics.

Q What educational degree does Tom Scholz, founder and guitar player for the band Boston, have?

A Master's degree in mechanical engineering from the Massachusetts Institute of Technology.

Did you know?

Besides boasting a mechanical engineering degree from MIT, Tom Scholz was a product design engineer at Polaroid and inventor of the Rockman guitar amplifier.

Q What degree does Art Garfunkel, of Simon and Garfunkel fame, have?

A Master's degree in mathematics. He also spent a few years working on a PhD in mathematics but never finished.

➡ WHICH OF THE FOLLOWING BANDS HAVE NEVER HAD A NUMBER ONE HIT SONG ON THE *BILLBOARD* TOP 40 OR *BILLBOARD* HOT 100 SONG LISTS IN THE U.S.?

A Bruce Springsteen   E Kiss

B Led Zeppelin   G The Who

C Bob Marley   H Johnny Cash

D Bob Dylan   I The Grateful Dead

F James Brown   J The Ramones

ANSWER

Trick question. None of these bands had a Number One song on the charts.

Q What's the only one-chord song to break into the Top 10 U.S. Billboard charts?

A Nilsson Schmilsson's song "Coconut." Repeat after me, "She put de lime in de coconut, she drank dem bot up . . . "

Q Who wrote the lyrics to Johnny Cash's song "A Boy Named Sue"?

A The poet Shel Silverstein. The song was Cash's biggest hit on the U.S. *Billboard* Hot 100 chart, peaking at Number Two.

Q Who is the oldest performer to hit the U.K. singles charts?

A Louis Armstrong. He was 66 when "What a Wonderful World" was released in 1967.

Q Which Bruce Springsteen song came closest to earning him a Number One spot on the *Billboard* charts?

A "Dancing in the Dark," a 1984 single from the album *Born in the U.S.A.* The single spent four weeks on the charts in the Number Two spot.

>>>>>>>>>>>>> **Did you know?** <<<<<<<<<<<<<

Bruce Springsteen has never had a Number One hit, but don't pity him too much. Springsteen's 1984 album *Born in the U.S.A.* is tied with Michael Jackson's *Thriller* and Janet Jackson's *Rhythm Nation 1814* for the most Top Ten singles from a single album (seven).

Q What two songs outranked Bruce Springsteen's "Dancing in the Dark" and prevented The Boss from earning a Number One *Billboard* hit?

A Prince's "When Doves Cry" and Duran Duran's "The Reflex." Prince? Fair enough. Duran Duran? So unfair.

Q Where did the band Duran Duran get its name?

A From a character in the 1968 film *Barbarella*. Dr. Durand Durand was the band's inspiration.

Q What actual event inspired the title of the 1984 Wham! song "Wake Me Up Before You Go-Go"?

A Band member Andrew Ridgeley left a note on the refrigerator to remind his mother to wake him up, but, in a drunken state, he penned the word "go" twice.

Q What was one of the songs temporarily banned by Clear Channel Communications, owner of 1,200+ radio stations in the United States, following the September 11, 2001, terrorist attacks?

A Louis Armstrong's "What a Wonderful World." Also banned were AC/DC's "Highway to Hell" and Billy Joel's "Only the Good Die Young."

Q What was the first song to hit Number One on the U.S. *Billboard* Hot 100 chart three separate times?

A "Le Freak'" by the band Chic. Its catchy refrain "Freak Out!" was originally "Fuck Off!"

Q What was the first song with a rap section to rank on the U.S. *Billboard* Hot 100 chart?

A Blondie's 1981 "Rapture."

Q What song has spent the most weeks at Number One on the *Billboard* Hot 100 chart?

A 1995's "One Sweet Day" by Mariah Carey and Boyz II Men. Sixteen weeks is a long time to be Number One, especially for a song as mediocre as that.

Q What song has spent the most total weeks on the *Billboard* Hot 100 chart?

A The 2012 song "Radioactive" by Imagine Dragons, with eighty-seven total weeks on the chart.

Q What band or musical artist has had the most Top Ten singles on the *Billboard* Hot 100 chart?

A Madonna, with thirty-eight singles, followed by Elvis Presley, The Beatles, and Michael Jackson.

Q Michael Jackson earned a patent for what in 1992 from the United States Patent and Trademark Office?

A Patent No. 5,255,452 granted Jackson and two partners a patent for "a method and means for creating anti-gravity illusion." Specifically the patent allows "a shoe wearer to lean forwardly beyond his center of gravity by virtue of wearing a specially designed pair of shoes which will engage with a hitch member movably projectable through a stage surface." Historical footnote: The patent expired in 2005 after the owners missed a payment. Duh!

Q How many stars on the Hollywood Walk of Fame does Michael Jackson have?

A Two. One for himself and one for his childhood band, The Jackson 5.

Q Mike Nesmith is famous as a member of the made-for-television band The Monkees. What is Mike's mother famous for?

A Inventing Liquid Paper.

Q What band played under the names Tea Set, Sigma 6, Screaming Abdabs, and Leonard's Lodgers?

A Pink Floyd.

Q What was the original name of the duo Sonny and Cher?

A Caesar and Cleo.

Q What musician played twenty-seven different instruments on his debut album, *For You*?

A Prince.

Q Who played the piano part on Bachman-Turner Overdrive's hit single "Takin' Care of Business"?

A The pizza delivery guy. He recorded his part in one take.

Q What band's backronym is Boys Entering Anarchic States Towards Internal Excellence?

A Beastie Boys.

According to Wikipedia, a backronym "is the same as an acronym, except that the meaning was created after the abbreviation."

Q The sole continuous member of what band is named Ian Fraser Kilmister?

A Motörhead's Lemmy.

Q What musician was married (and still is, as of this printing) at 1 a.m. at the 24-hour Always Forever Yours Wedding Chapel in Los Angeles, California?

A Tom Waits.

Q What television series did musician Iggy Pop appear in?

A *Star Trek: Deep Space 9*.

Q The Smith's guitarist Johnny Marr tried out for which English Premiere League soccer team as a teenager?

A Manchester City.

Q What band advertised for members with this job description: "Macho Types Wanted: Must Dance and Have a Moustache."

A The Village People.

Q What song has been performed by Fats Waller, Django Reinhardt, Louis Armstrong, Thelonious Monk, the Village People, and David Lee Roth?

A "Just a Gigolo."

Q What rock band did Chevy Chase's college bandmates later form?

A Steely Dan.

Q Which song is longer, MC Hammer's "2 Legit 2 Quit" or Pink Floyd's "Comfortably Numb"?

A "2 Legit 2 Quit," by more than ninety seconds.

Q What is the longest song ever recorded?

A "7 Skies H3" by the Flaming Lips. The song lasts for twenty-four hours. Only thirteen copies were released, each on a hard drive encased in a real human skull.

Q How much did it cost to purchase one of the thirteen original copies of the Flaming Lips' song "7 Skies H3"?

A $5,000. You can legally stream the song for free.

Q How many real albums from mock band Spinal Tap have ranked on the *Billboard* 200 list of top albums?

A Three. 1984's *This is Spinal Tap* (Number 121), 1992's *Break Like the Wind* (Number 61), and 2009's *Back from the Dead* (Number 52).

Q What was Spinal Tap's original name?

A The Originals.

Q What did The Originals change their name to, after discovering another band was called The Originals?

A The New Originals.

⮞ **WHICH OF THE FOLLOWING DID *NOT* KILL ONE OF SPINAL TAP'S TWELVE DRUMMERS?**

A̲ Bizarre gardening accident

B̲ Choking on somebody else's vomit

C̲ Abducted by aliens

D̲ Spontaneous combustion on stage

E̲ Accidentally packed away with the band's equipment and never seen again

ANSWER
C. The rest are authentically fictional, or fictionally authentic, causes of death listed for Spinal Tap's drummers.

Q How did Joy Division's lead singer, Ian Curtis, kill himself?

A Hanged in the kitchen with a clothesline.

Q What did the coroner list as the official cause of death for Rolling Stones guitarist Brian Jones, found dead at the bottom of a swimming pool?

A "Death by misadventure."

1	Vic Chesnutt	A	Shotgun to head
2	Kurt Cobain	B	Overdose of muscle relaxants
3	Darby Crash	C	Strangled by own belt
4	Michael Hutchence	D	Self-inflicted gunshot wound
5	Wendy O Williams	E	Two stabs wounds to own chest
6	Elliot Smith	F	Intentional heroin overdose

ANSWERS

1B, 2A, 3F, 4C, 5D, 6E

Q The dinosaur *Masiakasaurus knopfleri* is named after what musician?

A Mark Knopfler.

Q How old was Mandy Smith when Rolling Stones bassist Bill Wyman, age 48, began dating her?

A 13.

Q How old was Mandy Smith when she and Bill Wyman were married?

A 18.

Q How old was Mandy Smith when she and Bill Wyman were divorced?

A 18.

Q When Bill Wyman's son later married Mandy Smith's mother, what was the son's new relationship to Mandy?

A He became a stepfather to his former stepmother.

Q What musician's child was frequently babysat by Andy Warhol?

A Mick Jagger's daughter Jade.

Q What actor/singer babysat the Red Hot Chili Peppers' Anthony Kiedis?

A Cher.

Q What singer babysat the young Keanu Reeves?

A Alice Cooper.

Q Besides being famous for macabre live stage performances, what else is Alice Cooper noted for?

A Being a semi-pro golfer and a frequent contestant on *The Hollywood Squares* game show. It's no joke to say that Alice Cooper is the first glam-rock star to film serious television ads for golf clubs.

>>>>>>>>>>>>>> **Did you know?** <<<<<<<<<<<<

Spotify's list of the most misquoted songs of all time includes Jimi Hendrix's "Purple Haze" ('scuse me, while I kiss this guy), Elton John's "Tiny Dancer" (hold me closer, Tony Danza), and The Clash's "Rock the Casbah" (rock the cat box).

Q Ricky Raphel Brown (aka NoClue) holds a place in *The Guinness Book of World Records* for what?

A The "Fastest Rap MC" for rapping 723 syllables in just over fifty-one seconds.

Q How many "fa's" and "la's" does the Christmas song "Deck the Halls" feature?

A Twelve "fa's" and ninety-six "la's." It reached Number 61 on the U.S. *Billboard* Hot 100 chart as performed by the country band SheDAISY.

Q What does the word "karaoke" mean in Japanese?

A "Empty orchestra." The first karaoke machines were built in 1971 by Japanese musician Daisuke Inoue. He was tired of playing in a back-up band for Japanese businessmen who craved sing-a-longs to pop and traditional Japanese folk songs.

Q When was the first cassette tape created?

A 1963, by Philips Electronics.

Q In what year did Sony sell its first Walkman cassette-tape music player?

A 1979.

Q When was the MP3 invented?

A The digital-audio compression standard MP3 was developed in the early 1990s and launched commercially in 1993. The computer program Winamp debuted in 1998 and was the very first free MP3 player.

Q What was the marketing tagline of Apple's first iPod when it was released in 2001?

A "1,000 songs in your pocket." Not bad for a device equipped with a not-so-large 5 gigabyte hard drive.

Karaoke Dreamin'

Do you dream of a career as a karaoke pop star? Do you yearn to compcte for the title of world's best cover crooner? If that describes you, consider starting with one of the following sure-fire hit songs. They are the Top Ten karaoke songs of all time, based on royalty collections:

1 "Waterloo" by Abba

2 "Bohemian Rhapsody" by Queen

3 "My Way" by Frank Sinatra

4 "I Will Survive" by Gloria Gaynor

5 "Dancing Queen" by Abba

6 "Angels" by Robbie Williams

7 "Like a Virgin" by Madonna

8 "It's Raining Men" by Weather Girls

9 "Summer Nights" by Olivia Newton John and John Travolta

10 "I Should Be So Lucky" by Kylie Minogue

FAMOUS INVENTIONS

Famous Inventions

Q When were the very first patents granted?

A In Venice in the 1450s. The world's first patents were granted to protect glassblowers from competitors copying their designs.

Q When was the first patent issued in the United States?

A 1790. It was issued to Samuel Hopkins for a process to make potash, an ingredient used in fertilizer.

Q What government official signed that very first U.S. patent, in 1790?

A None other than President George Washington.

Q How many patents were issued in the United States in the first three years of the United States Patent & Trademark Office (USPTO)?

A Fewer than sixty patents.

Q How many patents have since been issued by the USPTO?

A More than 9.6 million and counting.

POP QUIZ

George Washington

1 Did George Washington wear false teeth made of wood?

2 How many real teeth did George Washington have when he was inaugurated president in 1789?

3 On Inauguration Day, what were George Washington's false teeth made from?

4 How many patents were awarded to George Washington?

ANSWERS

1 No. Never.

2 One.

3 Hippopotamus ivory and real human teeth.

4 None. Though a later figure named George Constant Louis Washington did acquire twenty-six patents, including one for instant coffee.

Patent protection runs deep in the United States. Article I, Section 8, of the U.S. Constitution states that "Congress shall have power . . . to promote the progress of science and useful arts, by securing for limited times to authors and inventors the exclusive right to their respective writings and discoveries."

This led to the 1790 U.S. Patent Act, which established what today is known as the United States Patent & Trademark Office (USPTO). To receive a patent in the early days, you needed approval from at least two of the following: secretary of state, secretary of war, attorney general.

The USPTO issues three types of patents:

1 Utility patents cover new and useful processes, machines, or compositions of matter. You can also acquire a utility patent for discovering a new and useful improvement to any of the above.

2 Design patents cover new, original, and ornamental designs for a manufactured article.

3 Plant patents are awarded for the invention or discovery of a new and distinct variety of plant that can be asexually reproduced.

Since 1995, utility and plant patents are granted for twenty years. Design patents last fourteen years.

Q When was sliced bread invented?

A 1928. That's when sliced bread received patent protection. It was soon marketed under the Kleen Maid Sliced Bread brand. The inventor of sliced bread, Otto Frederick Rohwedder of Iowa, spent sixteen years developing his bread-slicing machine. Most bakers were highly skeptical that a machine could evenly slice bread. Rohwedder's machine not only sliced bread, it also wrapped sliced loaves in paper and tied them up with a string.

Q Is actress Betty White older than sliced bread?

A Yes. Betty White was born in 1922, six years before the very first loaf of bread was mechanically sliced.

 **Did you know?**

The first mechanically sliced loaf sold under the famous Wonder Bread brand was sold in 1930.

Q What did the United States government ban in 1943?

A Sliced bread. The U.S. government claimed the ban would save paper and help the war effort since, unlike whole loaves, sliced loaves had to be wrapped in paper for transport. The unpopular ban lasted less than two months!

Which of the following are real patents issued by the USPTO?

1 Animal ear protectors. A device to protect the ears of animals from being soiled by food while the animal is eating. It consists of a tubular member for containing and protecting each ear, and a member to position the tubular member and animal ears away from the mouth and food of the animal while it is eating.

2 Device for the treatment of hiccups. A method and apparatus involving galvanic stimulation of the superficial, phrenetic, and vagus nerves using an electric current, intended to stop hiccups in the apparatus's wearer.

3 Apparatus for simulating a "high five." A device with a lower arm, a simulated hand, an upper arm, an elbow joint, and a spring element for biasing the upper and lower arms toward a predetermined alignment.

4 Anti-eating face mask. A cup-shaped device placed over the mouth and chin to block food from entering the wearer's mouth.

5 Apparatus for harnessing wind to drive a bicycle. A sail attached above the back wheel of a bicycle that harnesses wind to drive the bicycle forward.

6 Dust cover for a dog. A zip-up suit for a dog intended to enhance the efficacy of flea and pest treatments applied to the animal. The suit is intended to be air tight, with only the animal's mouth and nose exposed.

7 Soup bowl attraction. A simulated soup bowl entertainment attraction. It includes a large, bowl-shaped contrivance, a fog generator to produce a fog layer at the top of the bowl-shaped contrivance, and an imaging device producing an image viewable from a position looking down into the top of the bowl-shaped contrivance.

8 Nuclear war group-survival structures and campsite. Structures on a campsite built to protect people inside from the blast of the nuclear explosion. The sheltering structures are interlinked to provide a quasi-normal indoor way of life during the period of necessary confinement, up to several weeks. During peacetime, the structures can be used as camping facilities.

9 Novelty sunglasses with information-display members having the form of moose antlers. What more can be said?

ANSWER

All are real.

Q When was carbonated water invented?

A 1733, by Joseph Priestley. The Englishman invented carbonated water not as a fun and fizzy way to consume sugar water, but as a way to treat sailors for scurvy. Whoops.

➤ **WHICH OF THE FOLLOWING ITEMS WAS *NOT* DISCOVERED OR INVENTED IN THE 1800S?**

A Coffee pot	F Fax machine
B Roller skates	G Zippers
C Yale door lock	H Penicillin
D Ballpoint pen	I Gasoline-powered car
E Ice machine	J Barbed wire

ANSWER

H. Penicillin was a twentieth-century innovation, discovered in 1928 by Scottish scientist Alexander Fleming. Everything else on the list was discovered or invented in the nineteenth century.

Q Was the fax machine really invented in the nineteenth century?

A Yes, even the fax machine. It was invented in 1843 by Alexander Bain. His version used synchronized pendulums and electrochemically sensitive paper to scan a document and then send and reproduce it over copper wires.

Q Who invented the first disposable razor blade?

A King Camp Gillette. And yes, that is his real name.

Gillette founded the American Safety Razor Company in 1901 (later renamed the Gillette Safety Razor Company) and began selling disposable razors to the public in 1903.

Q How many razors and blades did Gillette sell in his first year?

A Fifty-one razors and 168 blades.

Q How many razors did Gillette sell in his second year?

A More than ninety thousand razors and 123,000 blades. The infamous "sell cheap razors to increase demand for expensive replacement blades" business model had finally arrived!

Q What patented men's overalls were originally marketed under the line, "It's no use, they can't be ripped"?

A Levi's jeans. The first jeans were invented by Jacob Davis and Levi Strauss, using fabric from Strauss's store in San Francisco, California, and metal rivets from Davis' shop in Reno, Nevada. The idea was to put rivets at places where pants typically tore—pocket corners and the base of the button fly. In 1873, Davis and Strauss earned a patent for "an improvement in fastening-pocket openings."

Q What were Levi Strauss's pants originally called?

A Originally they were branded *XX* and called "overalls." In 1890, the overalls were given the lot number "501," a name that has stuck ever since. It wasn't until 1960 that the name "jeans" came into fashion.

Q Where does the name "denim" come from?

A The fabric used in the first Levi jeans was an indigo-dyed cotton fabric called denim, named after the French city of Nîmes. The fabric—originally called *serge de Nîmes* and later shortened—was first produced in Nîmes.

Did you know?

The Twinkie was invented in 1930 in Chicago. Its creator, James Dewar, noticed that the machines used to produce strawberry-filled shortcakes were idle for half the year when strawberries were out of season. His original recipe included a banana cream filling. The name was inspired by "Twinkle Toe Shoes."

Q How many Twinkies were sold each year in the early 1980s?

A Roughly 1 billion.

Q What's the recommended shelf life of a Twinkie?

A Forty-five days.

Name the Accidental Invention

What are the names of the following accidental inventions?

1 Discovered by a Swiss electrical engineer in 1948. After returning from a walk with his dog, he noticed something deeply tangled in the animal's fur. Eureka! He eventually named his invention after the French words *velours* (velvet) and *crochet* (hook) and earned a patent in 1955.

2 Swiss chemist Albert Hofmann, who was researching fungal compounds for medicinal uses, discovered this in 1943. It's derived from the fungus ergot, which commonly grows on wheat and rye plants. After accidentally ingesting some of his discovery, Hoffman had a nap—during which he experienced a kaleidoscope of images and colors in his dreams.

3 This began as medicine to treat high blood pressure. Early clinical trials showed the drug was ineffective, but one of its side effects caused the British scientists to launch a completely different clinical trial that was extremely successful. The drug was patented in 1996 and approved for use in the United States in 1998. Subsequent studies have shown it's effective at helping cut flowers stand up straight for a full week longer than their natural shelf life.

4 It breaks when stretched sharply, but also bounces and flows like a liquid. In science jargon it acts both like an elastic solid and a viscous liquid. It was accidentally discovered by scientists looking for a rubber substitute during World War II, when rubber was highly rationed.

5 The inventor of this was a U.S. Navy officer using springs to stabilize sensitive instruments aboard Navy ships. One of his experiments accidentally fell over and—voila! Two years later, in 1945, this item was demonstrated at the Gimbels department store in Philadelphia and proved to be an instant hit with shoppers.

6 It's made from flour, water, salt, mineral oils, and boric acid. It was developed by a soap manufacturer in the 1930s to clean dirty wallpaper but never caught on. When the company was facing bankruptcy in the 1950s, a nephew of the company's founder discovered it being used by kids at a local nursery school to make Christmas ornaments.

◆ **ANSWERS** ◆

1 Velcro

2 Lysergic acid diethylamide-25 (LSD)

3 Sildenafil (marketed in the U.S. as Viagra)

4 Silly Putty

5 Slinky

6 Play-Doh

TRUE OR FALSE? Between 1953 and 1973, the U.S. Central Intelligence Agency illegally dosed unsuspecting American citizens with LSD in an effort to develop truth serums and mind-controlling drugs for use against foreign spies.

TRUE.

TRUE OR FALSE? Heroin, marketed as a nonaddictive treatment for coughing fits and asthma, became a registered trademark of the German pharmaceutical company Bayer in 1898.

TRUE.

Heroin was also given to morphine addicts to ease their symptoms, even though heroin and morphine are closely related and equally addictive drugs.

TRUE OR FALSE? Aspirin was trademarked by Bayer in 1899.

TRUE.

The drug had been synthetically synthesized in 1897. It received a U.S. patent in 1900.

TRUE OR FALSE? The United States stripped Bayer of its trademarks for heroin and aspirin as part of the 1919 Treaty of Versailles, which Germany signed following its surrender in World War I.

TRUE.

The Treaty of Versailles also removed the drugs' trademarks in the United Kingdom, France, and Russia. The Aspirin trademark was left intact in more than eighty countries, including Canada and Germany.

Believe it or not: The following products started life as registered trademarks but are now considered "genericized trademarks" (essentially, not trademarks at all). Trademarks become generic over time if the majority of people think the name refers to a general class of product or service.

- Band-Aid: Invented in 1920 and trademarked by Johnson & Johnson. Easier to say than, "Mom, I need a self-adhesive bandage, please!"

- Bubble Wrap: The Sealed Air Corporation would prefer us all to call their product "air bubble packaging." Ain't gonna happen.

- Cellophane: Originally a trademark by DuPont. Still a registered trademark of Innovia Films Ltd. in Europe.

- Dry Ice: Remember the Dry Ice Corporation of America? Nope, few people do.

- Dumpster: A 1937 innovation by the Dempster Brothers. They called it the Dempster-Dumpster.

- Escalator: Coined by the Otis Elevator Company.

- Frisbee: The Wham-O company wishes its clever name for flying discs was a little less memorable.

- Granola: Also known as Granula. Both were registered trademarks in the early twentieth century.

- Jacuzzi: Invented by Candido Jacuzzi, one of seven Jacuzzi brothers, in 1948.

- Jeep: Trademarked in 1943 by Willys-Overland. The lower-case "jeep" can refer to any four-wheel drive suited to rugged terrain.

- Popsicle: A trademark on the verge of genericization. Unilever would like us all to believe that popsicles are not synonymous with frozen treats on a stick. They also want you to know that, "It is not correct to say 'I'd like a Popsicle.' It is correct to say 'I'd like a Popsicle® ice pop.'"

- Styrofoam: Extruded polystyrene foam insulation. That's a mouthful. No wonder the Dow Chemical Company's trademark for STYROFOAM™ no longer includes disposable coffee cups and the like.

- Thermos: The German company Thermos GmbH lost its trademark for Thermos brand vacuum flasks in 1963.

- Touch-Tone: A former trademark of AT&T.

- Trampoline: Invented and popularized in the 1940s by gymnast George Nissen. By the 1980s, his trademark was toast.

- Videotape: Originally trademarked by the Ampex Corporation.

- Webster's Dictionary: Only the Merriam-Webster dictionary is trademarked; anybody else can legally publish a so-called Webster's Dictionary.

- Yo-Yo: If you're Canadian, the Papa's Toy Co. Ltd. owns your Yo-Yo trademark. In the United States, it became a plain old yo-yo in 1965.

- Zipper: Trademarked by the B.F. Goodrich Company in 1923.

    Generic trademarks are not much use to their owners. That's why companies try hard not to become the de facto name for their product or service, much like these trademarks on the threshold of genericization:

- Chapstick
- Kleenex
- Google
- Plexiglass
- Jumbotron

Q What was the very first Frisbee called?
A Whirlo-Way.

Q What was the Frisbee's second name?
A Flyin-Saucer.

Q What was the Frisbee's third name?
A Pluto-Platter.

Q In what year did the Frisbee become the Frisbee?

A 1958.

⟫⟫⟫⟫ **A Brief History of the Flying Disc** ⟪⟪⟪⟪

The first modern "flying disc" was invented in 1947 by
Fred Morrison under the name Whirlo-Way. In 1948,
Morrison and his business partner, Warren Franscioni,
redesigned and remarketed the disc under the name
Flyin-Saucer, inspired by the 1947 UFO sightings in
Roswell, New Mexico. Each disc came with a "space
license" and—as a joke—with 100-foot rolls of invisible
wire to keep the novel disc flying. Get it? Rolls of
invisible wire. Ha ha.

In 1955, the disc was renamed the Pluto-Platter.
Wham-O acquired the rights to the Pluto-Platter in
1957; Morrison earned a patent for his work in 1958.
The same year, Wham-O's new head of marketing
learned that college students in New England were
calling the Pluto-Platter the Frisbee, in honor of the
Frisbie Pie Company in Connecticut. The name stuck.

Nowadays "Frisbee" is a borderline generic term for
any type of flying disc. Of course, the Wham-O toy
company would prefer you to use its trademarked
name—that's Frisbee with a capital "F," if you please.

A 1940s
C 1960s

B 1950s
D 1970s

ANSWER

B. The Wham-O company trademarked the Hula Hoop in 1958. A few years later, U.S. Patent Number 3,079,728 was granted to the company for a hoop toy "fabricated from an extruded tubular member which is then formed into a substantially rigid closed loop." Wow, that sounds like so much fun.

➤ IN WHAT DECADE WAS THE LEGO INTERLOCKING BRICK INVENTED?

A 1940s
C 1960s

B 1950s
D 1970s

ANSWER

B. The Lego Group was founded in Denmark in the 1930s (the name means "play well" in Danish). The company's famous interlocking brick appeared in 1958.

➤ IN WHAT DECADE WERE TINKERTOYS INVENTED?

A 1890s
C 1910s

B 1900s
D 1920s

ANSWER

C. Charles Pajeau founded the Toy Tinkers Company and introduced Tinkertoys—wooden sticks that can be inserted into wooden dowels and wheels to build all sorts of structures—in 1914. The man was clearly a marketing genius: To promote the toys during the Christmas season, Pajeau hired elves (e.g., little people) to play with Tinkertoys in department store windows.

➤ **IN WHAT DECADE WAS THE RUBIK'S CUBE INVENTED?**

A 1960s   C 1980s

B 1970s   D 1990s

ANSWER.

> B. Ernő Rubik, a Hungarian architecture professor, invented his twisting puzzle in 1974. In the 1980s, the cube became internationally famous.

 **Did you know?**

> Pop star Justin Beiber can solve the Rubik's Cube in eighty-four seconds. That's fast, but not as fast as the current world record held by Mats Valk of the Netherlands. In 2013, he solved the Rubik's Cube in a hard-to-believe 5.55 seconds. The fastest time for solving the cube with your feet—yes, your feet—is an equally hard-to-believe 25.14 seconds, set by Gabriel Campanha of Brazil in 2014.

TRUE OR FALSE? The first country to "achieve space" and send something beyond Earth's atmosphere was Nazi Germany.

TRUE.

> And surprising. Maybe you were thinking the Russians or Americans got there first? In reality, Adolf Hitler's V2 rocket program sent the first manmade object into space in 1942, nearly fifteen years before Russia's *Sputnik* satellite was put into orbit.

1	Heinrich Hertz	A	The first bicycle, the two-wheeled *Laufmaschine*, in 1819
2	Manfred von Ardenne	B	Aspirin and heroin
3	Karl Friedrich von Drais	C	Television (he also broadcast the Olympics in 1936)
4	Johann Philipp Reis	D	The electromagnetic theory of light and electromagnetic waves
5	Karlheinz Brandenburg	E	The first programmable computer, in 1941
6	Gottlieb Daimler	F	The internal-combustion engine for automobiles
7	Konrad Zuse	G	The first telephone
8	Amalie Auguste Melitta Bentz	H	MP3 music-compression technology
9	Felix Hoffmann	I	The coffee filter
10	Fritz Pfleumer	J	Magnetic audiotape

278

ANSWERS

1D, 2C, 3A, 4G, 5H, 6F, 7E, 8I, 9B, 10J. Extra credit: They're all German except for Pfleumer, the inventor of audiotape. He was born in Salzburg, Austria.

TRUE OR FALSE? Nobody is certain who invented the modern fire hydrant, because the original patent for the fire hydrant burned in a fire.

TRUE.

The head of Philadelphia's water department, Frederick Graff Sr., is credited with inventing the modern fire hydrant—the one you see on most street corners with screw-on plugs and a dome—in 1801. It's more than a little ironic that an 1836 fire at the U.S. Patent Office destroyed the patent and its original inventor's identity.

TRUE OR FALSE? The world's first portable fire extinguisher, patented in 1723, contained a central chamber filled with gunpowder.

TRUE.

Ambrose Godfrey invented a fire extinguisher that used fuses and gunpowder to literally explode and disperse a fire-extinguishing liquid. As they say, fight fire with fire.

TRUE OR FALSE? The world's first emergency telephone hotline was pioneered in the United Kingdom in 1937.

TRUE.

The number was—and still is—999. The United States's national emergency number, 911, was introduced in 1968.

TRUE OR FALSE? The American Dental Association (ADA) considered the first fluoride toothpastes in 1937 to be dangerous, unscientific, and irrational.

TRUE.

At the time, the ADA was uncomfortable with the potential toxicity of fluoride.

TRUE OR FALSE? The Colgate-Palmolive company received a patent in 1990 for dispensing two differently colored stripes of toothpaste from a tube.

TRUE.

The patent is for a "multicolor surface striping device" that pumps out colorful blobs of paste onto your toothbrush. A completely different patent covers "simultaneous coextrusion of two or more flowable materials in a predetermined proportion." In other words, your two-in-one and three-in-one toothpastes (think: Aquafresh) are a completely different technology than your striped toothpastes (think: Colgate).

TRUE OR FALSE? The first commercial use of nylon, a synthetic fiber invented by the DuPont Company in 1935, was in a toothbrush.

TRUE.

A toothbrush with nylon bristles was sold to the public for the first time in 1938.

TRUE OR FALSE? After toothbrush bristles, nylon's next commercial success was in women's stockings.

TRUE.

They call them "nylons" for a reason.

TRUE OR FALSE? During World War II, DuPont stopped producing nylon stockings and retooled its factories to make nylon ropes and parachutes for the U.S. military.

TRUE.

DuPont stopped making women's nylon stockings in 1942. When the war ended, DuPont had difficulty meeting demand for its products, leading to the so-called "Nylon Riots" of 1945 and '46 when hundreds of women across the U.S. were injured and arrested in semi-violent brawls over scarce supplies of nylons.

TRUE OR FALSE? Kevlar is the world's strongest synthetic fiber.

TRUE.

Kevlar, also invented by DuPont, is stronger than steel and can hold up to 520,000 pounds per square inch. If you weighed 52 pounds, the strand of Kevlar needed to support your weight would measure just $1/10,000$ of a square inch across.

TRUE OR FALSE? Spider silk is stronger than Kevlar.

TRUE.

Spider silk has tensile strength (the amount of stretching a material can withstand before breaking) greater than both steel and Kevlar.

TRUE OR FALSE? Carbon nanotube fibers are even stronger than spider silk.

TRUE.

These revolutionary fibers are spun into textile threads that can be used to produce bulletproof clothing and body armor. Just be warned that carbon nanotube fibers conduct heat and electricity extremely well.

TRUE OR FALSE? The animated GIF is pronounced "jif" and is named after the Jif brand of peanut butter.

TRUE.

Get over it. It's a soft "jif" and not a hard "gif."

TRUE OR FALSE? The iPhone would cost roughly $5 million in 1975 dollars.

MOSTLY TRUE.

In 1975, the fastest supercomputers cost about $5 million. Today's iPhones offer roughly the same amount of computing power for a fraction of the price.

Three Inventions that Changed the World

According to the research firm McKinsey, these general-purpose technologies have had the largest impact on the modern world.

1 The development of steel. It's stronger and lighter than its predecessor, iron. But it wasn't until Henry Bessemer figured out how to efficiently remove impurities from steel in 1855 that it became a mass-produced and relatively inexpensive—and essential—material. Without cheap steel we wouldn't have built intercontinental trains, all sorts of tools, skyscrapers, cars, razor blades, and—gasp!—stainless-steel gravy boats.

2 The printing press. In Western Europe the movable-type press was made famous by Johannes Gutenberg in 1450. Originally built as a way to make accurate copies of the Bible, Gutenberg's printing press quickly found applications in science, academia, and the military. The printing press is credited with sparking the Enlightenment and laying the foundation for mass communication across borders and cultures.

3 The electric motor. It was a major improvement over the steam- and water-powered engines it eclipsed, in part because factories were no longer tied to organizing workspaces and manufacturing processes around a central power conduit. Electric engines revolutionized not just factories but also the home—every modern convenience in your kitchen relies on an electric motor.

DEATH

. CHAPTER 13 .

Death

TRUE OR FALSE? You are 14 percent more likely to die on your own birthday, compared to any other day of the year.

_____
TRUE.

It's a bit morbid, but your "special day" increases your odds of dying from a fall (often alcohol-related), by suicide, or from a stroke or heart attack due to the stress of celebration. You're in good company if it happens to you. William Shakespeare (April 23), Ingrid Bergman (August 29), and Hawaii's King Kamehameha V (December 11) all died on their birthdays.

TRUE OR FALSE? More than 135,000 people will die on your next birthday.

_____
TRUE.

It's OK to celebrate the 360,000 people who will be born on your next birthday. Just give a kind thought to the 135,000 people who will pass away on the same day.

TRUE OR FALSE? Monday is the most popular day to commit suicide.

FALSE.

Wednesday, by far, is the most popular day to commit suicide. So much for hating Mondays!

TRUE OR FALSE? More people die in New York City each year from murder than from suicide.

FALSE.

Murder is not your problem. The City that Never Sleeps has a way of making you do yourself in.

TRUE OR FALSE? More people jump to their deaths from New York's Brooklyn Bridge than any other bridge in North America.

FALSE.

San Francisco's Golden Gate Bridge is the most popular "suicide bridge" in North America. The official death count was halted just before it reached one thousand deaths in order to avoid a macabre contest of trying to be the thousandth suicide jumper.

TRUE OR FALSE? You're unlikely to kill yourself by attempting suicide.

TRUE.

Fewer than one in twenty-five suicide attempts are successful—unless you're an old fart, in which case one in four suicide attempts are successful.

TRUE OR FALSE? The most common method of suicide in the United States is death by gunshot.

TRUE.

Second best are suffocation (often from carbon monoxide poisoning) and straight-up poisoning (often from drug overdoses).

TRUE OR FALSE? You have a higher chance of being killed by a donkey than of dying in a plane crash.

TRUE.

Believe it or not, 96 percent of people involved in a plane crash survive.

TRUE OR FALSE? You're more likely to die from a dog bite than from the bite of a bat or ferret.

FALSE.

You are five times more likely to die from the bite of a bat or ferret than from the bite of a domesticated dog. The bite of a wild dog? You're on your own.

 **Did you know?**

Struck on the head by a coconut? That's the cause of death for about 150 people each year.

TRUE OR FALSE? You're slightly more likely to die from a cave-in than from contact with hot tap water.

TRUE.

If you're stuck in that cave-in, be warned there's an additional one in 2.5 million chance that you will actually die caught between the proverbial rock and hard spot. It's certainly a poetic way to go.

TRUE OR FALSE? You're slightly more likely to die from your pajamas catching fire than from the bite of a venomous spider.

TRUE.

TRUE OR FALSE? You're slightly more likely to drown in a bathtub than to die from electrocution.

TRUE.

TRUE OR FALSE? For humans, the most deadly animals on the planet are snakes.

FALSE.

There's no contest here—mosquitos cause the most human deaths, more than 725,000 per year. It's because mosquitos spread disease, the worst of which is malaria, which alone is responsible for more than 600,000 deaths each year. Mosquitos also spread deadly diseases such as dengue and yellow fever and encephalitis. Snakes? They're third on the list, responsible for about fifty thousand human deaths each year. Second on the list? Humans. Each year we kill 475,000 of our own.

TRUE OR FALSE? More people are killed each year by freshwater snails than by salt-water crocodiles.

TRUE.

Salt-water crocs are deadly and kill more than a thousand people each year. Freshwater snails are responsible for ten times as many deaths, however, thanks to parasitic worms. These infect the snails, which then spread the disease schistosomiasis in water sources used by humans.

TRUE OR FALSE? Each year more people are killed by hippopotamuses than by lions, sharks, and elephants combined.

TRUE.

Don't mess with hippos.

Playing the Odds

How are you likely to die? While it's normal to wonder what the end will be like, most people probably do not think it will come while playing a video game.

Here are the odds of being killed:

- While playing a video game: 100 million to one

- By venomous snake bite: 95 million to one

- By an asteroid falling to earth: 75 million to one

- By venomous spider bite: 25 million to one

- By champagne cork: 22 million to one

- By lightning: 10 million to one

- By bee or wasp sting: 5 million to one

- By falling down stairs: 157,000 to one

- By choking: 100,000 to one

- By heart disease: 467 to one

For a little perspective here, the odds of winning the California MEGA Millions lotto jackpot are one in 259 million.

A Guatemala   D Belize

B Venezuela   E El Salvador

C Honduras

ANSWER

C. Honduras. As of 2012, it had the highest murder rate on the planet. Venezuela is the second-most-deadly country. Rounding out the top five are Belize (oh no—it's not *always* better in Belize!), El Salvador, and Guatemala.

Q What was the only homicide-free country in 2012?

A Liechtenstein. You should also feel safe traveling in Iceland and Tonga, both of which reported just a single homicide in 2012.

C.13   DEATH

⟫⟫⟫⟫⟫⟫⟫⟫⟫   **Did you know?**   ⟪⟪⟪⟪⟪⟪⟪⟪⟪

In the United States, the homicide rate is relatively low at 4.7 per 100,000 people. This statistic, however, hides a gruesome truth: The U.S. population is large, so on a percentage basis, the murder rate appears low. In absolute numbers, more than 14,000 people were murdered in the U.S. in 2012.

Q Which job is more dangerous, airline pilot or construction worker?

A Pilot. Statistically speaking, more pilots die (roughly fifty-three per 100,000 pilots) compared with construction workers (seventeen per 100,000 workers).

Q Which job is more dangerous, roofer or commercial fisherman?

A Commercial fisherman. C'mon, don't you watch *Deadliest Catch*? The stats are 117 dead fisherman and forty dead roofers per 100,000 workers.

Q What is the most dangerous job in the United States?

A Logger. Climb trees and fell them with saws and axes. What could go wrong?

Q More than 70 percent of serious injuries at American colleges and universities are caused by what sport?

A Cheerleading. Football is no picnic when it comes to injuries. But in the category of "catastrophic injuries" requiring visits to an emergency room, cheerleading is far more dangerous. Concussions are the most common cheer-related injury. And yes, cheerleading is definitely a sport (see the *Ultimate Book of Sports* if you don't believe).

Q What is the deadliest road in the world?

A Not totally a fair question, as there's no single source of data. That said, most people agree that Bolivia's Yungas Road (aka El Camino de la Muerte, or Road of Death), Afghanistan's Kabul-Jalalabad Road, and Pakistan's Karakoram Highway are among the most deadly.

Q Which drug is more dangerous, LSD or ecstasy?

A LSD, if you're judging based on harm done to individuals or to society and whether the drug induces dependence.

Q How many deaths from marijuana overdose were there in 2010 in the United States?

A Zero.

Q Which drug is more dangerous, alcohol or tobacco?

A Tobacco. More than 443,000 people in the United States die each year from smoking-related diseases. Alcohol kills about 88,000 people each year from cirrhosis of the liver and other diseases linked to over-consumption of alcohol, as well as from accidents involving the use of alcohol. Excessive drinking also leads to more than a million emergency room visits each year.

Q Which drug is more dangerous, heroin or cocaine?

A Heroin. It's ranked as the world's most dangerous drug. More than three thousand people overdosed on heroin in the United States in 2010.

Q What's the deadliest substance known to science?

A Type "H" botulinum toxin. It's the first new botulinum protein discovered in more than forty years, and it is so potent that 13 billionths of a gram can kill an adult. Scientists are so concerned about its toxicity that—for the first time—the protein's DNA sequence has been withheld from public databases due to security concerns.

C. *botulinum*, the bacterium that produces the toxic type "H" botulinum, also produces the key ingredient in the anti-wrinkle treatment Botox.

Q What was the deadliest accident in commercial aviation?

A The 1977 collision of KLM flight 4805 and Pan Am flight 1736 in Tenerife, Canary Islands. A bomb explosion on the ground forced numerous planes to divert to Los Rodeos airport; bad weather and poor air-traffic communications caused the two Boeing 747s to crash on the runway, killing 583 passengers and crew.

Q What's the deadliest natural disaster since 1900?

A The flooding of China's Yangtze River in 1931. More than 5 feet of rain fell over a three-month period, flooding China's Yangtze and Huai rivers. China's capital at the time, Nanjing, was devastated. Over the course of five months, nearly 3.7 million people died from direct and indirect impacts of the floods.

➤ HOW MANY PEOPLE DIED WHEN THE BANQIAO AND SHIMANTAN DAMS IN CHINA FAILED IN 1979?

A More than 1,500   C More than 150,000

B More than 15,000   D More than 1.5 million

ANSWER
C. At least 170,000 people died when rainfall overwhelmed the dams, causing them to burst.

2004 Indian Ocean Earthquake and Tsunami

Everything about the world's fifth-deadliest natural disaster, in 2004, was massive. It started with a 9.1 magnitude earthquake in Indonesia. The quake is the third largest ever recorded and lasted a record-breaking eight minutes. The ensuing tsunami, also the largest ever recorded, killed more than 230,000 people in fifteen countries. More than 1.5 million people were displaced. Waves peaked at more than 100 feet high and reached up to 1.2 miles inland.

Q Where was the deadliest blizzard in modern times?

A Iran. More than four thousand people died in the 1972 Iran blizzard. Up to 26 feet of snow fell in parts of southern Iran.

Q Where was the deadliest earthquake in modern times?

A China. The 1976 Tangshan earthquake in northern China killed approximately 272,000 people (official estimate) or more than 600,000 people (independent estimates).

Q How many people died in the deadliest heat wave in modern history, in 2003?

A More than seventy thousand.

A Northern Africa

B Southern Europe

C Western United States

D Australia

ANSWER

B. Much of France and southern Europe bore the brunt of the 2003 heat wave.

Did you know?

The Black Death is history's most deadly verifiable plague. It swept through Europe and Asia Minor in the 1340s and '50s, killing an estimated 25 percent to 60 percent of Europe's population.

Q What's the deadliest industrial disaster in modern times?

A The 1984 Bhopal catastrophe. More than forty-five tons of poisonous gas leaked from a Union Carbide plant in Bhopal, India. Thousands of people died instantly, and hundreds more died in the ensuing panic as people attempted to evacuate Bhopal. The final death toll is estimated at twenty thousand people, with an additional 500,000 people injured or suffering long-term health consequences from gas exposure.

Boston's Great Molasses Disaster

While it does not win the title of "worst industrial disaster," the 1919 molasses disaster in Boston is certainly one of history's most gruesome industrial accidents.

Molasses is a by-product of producing refined sugar from cane or beets. Molasses is thick and syrupy stuff, and it retains heat well. So it was an epic disaster when a tanker loaded with 2.3 million gallons of molasses burst open in Boston's North End in 1919. Reports from the time say a 25-foot-tall wall of molasses flowed through Boston's streets at more than 35 miles per hour. Dozens of buildings were destroyed and more than twenty people were killed.

What's worse? The temperature of the molasses was warm enough to gently cook the flesh of people and horses that were snared in the quicksand-like substance.

No surprise, it took months to clean the streets of Boston. For years after, locals complained that the air stank of molasses on hot summer days.

Q What's the deadliest epidemic in modern history?

A The Spanish Flu. A virulent strain of influenza known as H1N1 spread throughout Asia, Europe, and North America in the spring of 1918 during the final months of World War I. Healthy adults were especially hard hit. The global death toll is estimated between 25 million and 100 million.

=== **Deadly Disasters** ===

Which of the following deadly disasters actually happened?

1 Two people were killed and more than thirty were injured in 2006 when a bouncy castle in England snapped its moorings and floated away, carried by strong winds.

2 George Herbert, the fifth Earl of Carnarvon and the financial backer behind the excavation of Tutankhamun's tomb, died after he accidentally cut a mosquito bite on his face while shaving in 1923. The cut became infected, leading to blood poisoning and eventually pneumonia. Apparently that's what happens when you're cursed by a pharaoh!

3 At a music club in Rhode Island, more than four hundred people were trapped when pyrotechnic sparks ignited the stage. In the ensuing panic to get out, all exits were clogged with people. Some emergency doors were chained shut. The club burned to the ground in less than six minutes. More than a hundred people died.

4 Isadora Duncan, a famous dancer, died when her long flowing scarf caught in the rear axle of the car she was in. Her neck was instantly broken.

5 The largest known mass asphyxiation happened when a pocket of carbon dioxide gas erupted from the depths of Lake Nyos in Cameroon. Everything within a fifteen-mile radius of the lake was killed—including more than 1,700 people—as all breathable air was pushed away by the cloud of toxic gas, causing mass suffocation.

6 Mike Edwards, cellist for the 1970s band ELO, was killed by a hay bale that rolled down a hill and smashed into his moving van.

7 Health advocate Basil Brown consumed ten gallons of carrot juice over a ten-day period in 1974. The cause of death was an overdose of Vitamin A.

8 Robert Williams is the first known person to be killed by a robot. He worked at a Ford automobile factory and was struck in the head by a robot in 1979.

9 Gary Hoy died when he fell to the ground from a building in Toronto, Canada, in 1993. He was proving that the glass was unbreakable. The glass did not break when he ran into it, but it did separate from the windowpane.

ANSWER

They are all real.

George Herbert—the amateur Egyptologist and unlucky fellow who died from shaving—owned Highclere Castle, setting for the *Downton Abbey* television drama. Herbert's descendants, along with many rare pieces from the Tutankhamen excavation, still reside at Highclere Castle.

Q In the United States, when was the last year that somebody officially died of "old age"?

A 1951. That's the last year "old age" was listed on death certificates. Nowadays it's referred to as "death by natural causes."

Q When you die, what's the last sense to fail?

A Hearing.

Q How many people have died in the history of the world?

A More than 100 billion, give or take a few million, since humans became a distinct species. That's the number estimated by scientists.

A "Dolores had no hobbies, made no contribution to society
and rarely shared a kind word or deed in her life. I speak for
the majority of her family when I say her presence will not be
missed by many, very few tears will be shed and there will be
no lamenting over her passing . . . All of us will really only miss
what we never had, a good and kind mother, grandmother and
great-grandmother. I hope she is finally at peace with herself.
As for the rest of us left behind, I hope this is the beginning of
a time of healing and learning to be a family again . . . There
will be no service, no prayers and no closure for the family she
spent a lifetime tearing apart."

B "Louis J. Casimir Jr. bought the farm Thursday, Feb. 5, 2004,
having lived more than twice as long as he had expected and
probably three or four times as long as he deserved. Although
he was born into an impecunious family, in a backward and
benighted part of the country at the beginning of the Great
Depression, he never in his life suffered any real hardships.
Many of his childhood friends who weren't killed or maimed
in various wars became petty criminals, prostitutes, and/or
Republicans. Lou was a daredevil: his last words were 'Watch
this!'"

C "Cynthia was a topless dancer who died performing an act
for which she was mildly famous: jumping out of a cake at a
bachelor's party. Unfortunately for Cynthia the cake she was
hiding within was well constructed and, quite apparently,

airtight. Cynthia suffocated inside the cake after waiting for more than 90 minutes to surprise the unsuspecting groom. In order for her death to mean anything, the family asks that, in future, topless dancers hiding inside cakes should not be made to wait for more than 5 minutes."

D "Jim, who had tired of reading obituaries noting other's courageous battles with this or that disease, wanted it known that he lost his battle. It was primarily as a result of being stubborn and not following doctor's orders or maybe for just living life a little too hard for better than five decades. He was sadly deprived of his final wish, which was to be run over by a beer truck on the way to the liquor store to buy booze for a date."

E "William Donaldson, who died on June 22 aged 70, was described by Kenneth Tynan as 'an old Wykehamist who ended up as a moderately successful Chelsea pimp,' which was true, though he was also a failed theatrical impresario, a crack-smoking serial adulterer and a writer of autobiographical novels; but it was under the nom de plume Henry Root that he became best known."

ANSWER
C.

A Create a certified, high-quality diamond from the cremated ashes of your loved one.

B Send a symbolic portion of your loved one's cremated remains into Earth orbit, onto the lunar surface, or into deep space.

C Have your cremated remains placed in a "reef ball" to help seed coral reefs.

D Have your remains frozen in liquid nitrogen, with the intent of restoring your body (in good health, of course) when technology becomes available to do so.

E Have your remains frozen and transformed into organic compost and buried within a potato-starch coffin that promotes plant and tree growth.

F Have your remains incorporated into fireworks, so you can have a custom fireworks display for your friends and loved ones.

G Create a custom portrait of your loved one incorporating their cremation ashes.

H Have your cremation ashes cut into a kilogram of premium Colombian cocaine and distributed on the streets of Southern California.

I Have your body mummified the old-school Egyptian way.

J Donate your body to be "plastinated," or embalmed for public display for educational and instructional purposes.

C.13 DEATH

303

ANSWER
    H. Nobody is getting high snorting your cremation ashes.

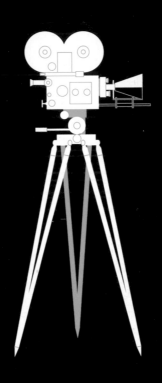

FILM

TELEVISION

Film & Television

Q What Hollywood producer wrote some early *Battlestar Galactica* episodes and created the television shows *Airwolf*, *JAG*, *Magnum P.I.*, *NCIS*, and *Quantum Leap*?

A Donald P. Bellisario.

Q Which fictional television character sported a moustache, a Detroit Tigers baseball cap, and a seemingly limitless supply of floral Hawaiian shirts?

A Thomas Magnum of *Magnum P.I.*

Q What was Thomas Magnum's full name?

A Thomas Sullivan Magnum IV.

Q What was the name of the estate where Thomas Magnum lived, as a guest?

A Robin's Nest.

Q What was the name of the estate's fussy caretaker?

A Jonathan Quayle Higgins III.

Q What were the names of Higgins' two Doberman pinschers responsible for patrolling the estate grounds?

A Zeus and Apollo.

Q What do the movies *A Few Good Men*, *The Social Network*, and *Moneyball* have in common?

A They were all written or adapted by Aaron Sorkin.

Q What was the name of the president in Aaron Sorkin's popular television show *The West Wing*?

A Josiah Bartlett.

➤ WHEN AARON SORKIN WAS ARRESTED IN 2001 AT BURBANK AIRPORT IN CALIFORNIA, WHAT ILLEGAL DRUG(S) WAS HE CARRYING IN HIS SUITCASES?

A Marijuana

B Crack cocaine

C Hallucinogenic mushrooms

D All of the above

ANSWER

D. When his crack pipe set off the metal detector at Burbank airport, security discovered all of the above in Sorkin's baggage.

Q Who produced the following (in)famous television shows: *Mod Squad, S.W.A.T., Charlie's Angels, The Love Boat, Fantasy Island, Hart to Hart, Starsky & Hutch, T.J. Hooker, Dynasty, Melrose Place, Beverly Hills, 90210, Twin Peaks,* and *Charmed*?

A Aaron Spelling.

Q What car did police detectives David Starsky and Kenneth Hutchison drive in the show *Starsky & Hutch*?

A 1974 Ford Gran Torino.

Q What was the name of Starsky and Hutch's confidential street informant?

A Huggy Bear.

Q What was the name of the accident-prone first mate on the television show *Gilligan's Island*?

A Willie Gilligan.

Q What was the name of the ill-fated boat that ran ashore in *Gilligan's Island*?

A The *S.S. Minnow*

Q Who was the *S.S. Minnow* named after?

A A former chairman of the Federal Communications Commission, Newton Minnow, who considered television to be a "vast wasteland."

Q What was the maiden name of Betty Rubble from the animated series *The Flintstones*?

A Betty Jean McBricker.

Q What was Wilma Flintstone's maiden name?

A Wilma Slaghoople.

Q What brand of cigarettes did Fred and Wilma smoke (in support of their show's sponsor, no doubt)?

A Winston.

Q In what year was the animated cartoon *The Jetsons* set?

A 2062.

Q In what year was the original *Star Trek* series set?

A The 2260s.

Q In what year is the show *Battlestar Galactica* set?

A Spoiler alert! Don't read this if you haven't seen the show. Seriously, stop reading. You have been warned. It's set in the year 148,000 BC. In other words, it's set about 150,000 years before the present day. Wow, dude, that's trippy.

Q When was the final episode of the original *Star Trek* series aired?

A 1969.

Q What year was the first *Star Trek* fan convention held?

A 1972.

Q What five other television series were spinoffs from the original *Star Trek*?

A *Star Trek: The Animated Series*, *Star Trek: The Next Generation*, *Star Trek: Deep Space Nine*, *Star Trek: Voyager*, and *Star Trek: Enterprise*.

Did you know?

The iconic mask used in the 1978 horror film *Halloween* was a plastic Captain Kirk mask from *Star Trek*, spray-painted white and with its eyeholes enlarged. Creepy!

Q What color is Spock's blood?

A Green. And not because he's an Irish leprechaun—it's because Vulcan blood includes copper, rather than iron, giving it a green sheen.

Q What percentage of all American households watched the final episode of *M*A*S*H** in 1983?

A Sixty percent. It remains the most-watched final episode in American television history.

Q Who is the only actress to have appeared in both *M*A*S*H** and *Star Trek*?

A Sally Kellerman. She appeared as Major Margaret "Hot Lips" Houlihan in Robert Altman's 1970 film *MASH* and as Dr. Elizabeth Dehner in the first season of the original *Star Trek* series.

Q   What famous phrase was *never* spoken in any *Star Trek* episode?

A   "Beam me up, Scotty."

➥ WHO SPOKE THE FOLLOWING FAMOUS CATCHPHRASES?

1   "I'll be back."

2   "Fascinating."

3   "I pity the fool."

4   "Kiss my grits!"

5   "Mmm, doughnuts."

6   "I love the smell of napalm in the morning."

7   "You talkin' to me?"

8   "Exterminate."

9   "Gentlemen, you can't fight in here! This is the War Room!"

10 "I'll get you, my pretty, and your little dog, too!"

A   Travis Bickle in *Taxi Driver*

B   Spock in *Star Trek*

C   Mr. T in *The A-Team*

D   President Merkin Muffley in *Doctor Strangelove*

E   Dalek in *Doctor Who*

F   Homer in *The Simpsons*

G   Arnold Schwarzenegger in *The Terminator*

H   Flo in *Alice*

I   Lt. Colonel Kilgore in *Apocalypse Now*

J   Wicked Witch of the West in *The Wizard of Oz*

ANSWERS
1G, 2B, 3C, 4H, 5F, 6I, 7A, 8E, 9D, 10J

Q   Who was originally considered for the leading role in the film *The Terminator*?

A   O.J. Simpson. Yes, *that* O.J. Simpson. Mel Gibson was also offered the role but turned it down. Arnold Schwarzenegger finally accepted.

Q How much did Arnold Schwarzenegger earn for each word he spoke in the publicly released version of *The Terminator*?

A Roughly $21,490 per word. Schwarzenegger was paid $15 million for the role and spoke seven hundred words.

Q What's the most frequently used word in the 1998 film *The Big Lebowski*?

A "Fuck." It's spoken 292 times. The word "dude" is spoken a mere 161 times. The word "man"? A scant 147 times.

Did you know?

The word "fuck" appears more than 265 times in the 1994 film *Pulp Fiction*, starring John Travolta and Samuel L. Jackson.

Q What is the most-watched television event in American history?

A Super Bowl XLVIII, despite the fact that the game itself was a suspense-free 48–3 blowout by the Seattle Seahawks over the Denver Broncos to end the 2013 professional football season.

Q What's the average cost for a thirty-second commercial during a Super Bowl?

A Roughly $4 million.

Q What's the highest-grossing movie of all time?

A Adjusted for inflation, it's the 1939 film *Gone with the Wind*, at roughly $3.3 billion.

Q What's the most expensive movie ever made?

A The 2009 film *Avatar*, which had a production budget of $425 million. Fortunately for the producers of *Avatar*, it ranks at Number Two on the list of highest-grossing films of all time, having earned an inflation-adjusted $2.7 billion since its 2009 release.

Q What is the most profitable movie of all time?

A The 2002 film *My Big Fat Greek Wedding*, which cost $6 million to produce and earned $369 million globally at the box office. Coming in a close second is the 2009 film *Paranormal Activity*, which cost $450,000 to produce and earned $89 million worldwide.

Q What is the least profitable major-studio film of all time?

A The 2011 film *Mars Needs Moms*, which lost $144 million. Not far behind are 2013's *The Lone Ranger* (lost $134 million) and 2012's *John Carter* (lost $131 million).

Q What film holds the record for consecutive weeks as the Number One film at the box office?

A *Titanic*, for a total of fifteen consecutive weeks. If you count total weeks at Number One, the film *E.T.* edges into first place, with sixteen total weeks at Number One.

Real or Fake Porn Films

Q

Which of the following pornographic movie titles are real and which are fake? If you know the correct answers, you have some explaining to do to your spouse, fiancé, girlfriend, or priest.

1 *Tiger's Wood*

2 *Edward Penishands*

3 *Assablanca*

4 *Schindler's Fist*

5 *Beverly Hills 9021-Ho!*

6 *Pulp Friction*

7 *Shaving Ryan's Privates*

8 *Forrest Hump*

9 *Indiana Bones and the Temple of Boobs*

10 *Raiders of the Lost Arse*

11 *Titty Titty Gang Bang*

12 *May the Foreskin Be With You*

13 *When Harry Met Harrier*

14 *Crack Whores of the Tenderloin*

15 *Girth, Wind & Fire*

16 *Turf Toe Hookers*

ANSWERS

1 True. The catchphrase? There are so many to choose from! "Dealing with tough lies," "In the rough," or "Get the most out of your woods," just to name a few.

2 True. Enough said.

3 False. But a great idea nonetheless.

4 False. Maybe not a great idea, but definitely a memorable title.

5 True.

6 True. Just don't tell Samuel L. Jackson.

7 Half true. This film exists, but it's a documentary about porn films that parody Hollywood films.

8 True.

9 True. And made by the same producer who created *Forrest Hump*.

Q What professional actor has earned the most money from acting?

A Samuel L. Jackson. He is estimated to have earned more than $7.4 billion from the 100+ movies he has appeared in. Actor Tom Hanks ranks Number Two on the same list, having earned more than $6.2 billion from his 40+ films.

Q What film has won the most Academy Awards?

A It's a three-way tie among *Ben Hur* (1952), *Titanic* (1997), and *Lord of the Rings: The Return of the King* (2003), each with eleven Oscars.

Q What are the only three films to have won all five major Oscars categories (Best Picture, Director, Screenplay, Actor, Actress)?

A *It Happened One Night* (1934), *One Flew over the Cuckoo's Nest* (1975), and *Silence of the Lambs* (1991)

⟫⟫⟫⟫⟫ **Take Your Award and Shove It** ⟪⟪⟪⟪⟪

Only two Academy Awards have been flat-out refused. The first was a Best Actor award given to George C. Scott in 1970 for his leading role in the film *Patton*. The actor cited his dislike of award competitions.

Marlon Brando took his Oscar refusal to an entirely new level. Brando won the Best Actor award for his role in the 1972 film *The Godfather* and, as a protest against the negative portrayal of Native Americans in movies, he sent a women calling herself Sacheen Littlefeather to refuse his award on his behalf, if such a thing is possible.

Many other actors have declined to accept their awards in person, including Woody Allen and Katharine Hepburn, both of whom are famously uninterested in walking down Oscar's red carpet.

Q Who has won the most Academy Awards?

A Walt Disney.

Q How many people have won the so-called EGOT: Emmy, Grammy, Oscar, and Tony awards?

A Twelve, including Audrey Hepburn, John Gielgud, Rita Moreno, Mel Brooks, and Whoopi Goldberg.

Q Which of the EGOT winners above also fought in the infamous Battle of the Bulge during World War II?

A Mel Brooks.

Q What's the title of the fake musical in Mel Brooks' 1968 film *The Producers*?

A *Springtime for Hitler: A Gay Romp with Adolf and Eva at Berchtesgaden.*

Q How many times was actor James Doohan (Scotty on *Star Trek*) shot during the D-Day landings in World War II?

A Six times.

Q Which army shot him?

A His own army, the Canadian Army.

Q Which actor has died in more films: Robert de Niro, Bruce Willis, or Johnny Depp?

A Robert de Niro, who's been killed in at least fourteen movies. Bruce Willis has died in eleven films, Johnny Depp in ten.

Celebrity Adoptions

Q

Which of the following celebrities were adopted as children and which celebrities have adopted children of their own?

1 Steve Jobs

2 Nicole Kidman

3 Debbie Harry

4 Marilyn Monroe

5 Angelina Jolie

6 Bill Clinton

7 Hugh Jackman

8 Gary Coleman

9 John Lennon

10 Mary-Louise Parker

ANSWERS

1 Adopted

2 Adoptive parent

3 Adopted

4 Adopted

5 Adoptive parent

6 Adopted

7 Adoptive parent

8 Adopted

9 Adopted

10 Adoptive parent

TRUE OR FALSE? Sex therapist Dr. Ruth Westheimer is a trained rifle sniper.

TRUE.

TRUE OR FALSE? George Lucas personally offered David Lynch the chance to direct *Star Wars: Return of the Jedi*, and Lynch flat-out refused.

TRUE.

TRUE OR FALSE? Nicolas Cage has owned more than fifteen mansions, a castle in Germany, a castle in England, and a private island in the Bahamas.

TRUE.

TRUE OR FALSE? Keanu Reeves was born in Lebanon.

TRUE.

TRUE OR FALSE? George Clooney bought a potbellied pig named Max for his former girlfriend Kelly Preston.

TRUE.

TRUE OR FALSE? When Kelly Preston left Clooney to date and marry actor John Travolta, Clooney got to keep the pig.

TRUE.

Clooney wanted the pig. Clooney got the pig.

Did you know?

George Clooney kept Max the potbellied pig for eighteen years, until Max died in 2006. That's dedication.

TRUE OR FALSE? Reese Witherspoon has two pet donkeys.

TRUE.

Their names are Honky and Tonky.

TRUE OR FALSE? Bruce Willis and Demi Moore were married in Las Vegas by singer Little Richard.

TRUE.

TRUE OR FALSE? Demi Moore was born Demetria Guynes.

TRUE.

TRUE OR FALSE? Donald Duck's middle name is Fauntleroy.

TRUE.

TRUE OR FALSE? Scoobert is the real name of Scooby-Doo.

TRUE.

TRUE OR FALSE? Shaggy's real first name is Shaggarath.

FALSE.

It's actually Norville.

TRUE OR FALSE? The original name of Mickey Mouse was Mortimer.

TRUE.

TRUE OR FALSE? The full name of Barbie (of doll fame) is Barbara Millicent Roberts.

TRUE.

TRUE OR FALSE? Oprah Winfrey was born Orpah Winfrey.

TRUE.

TRUE OR FALSE? Actor Albert Brooks, of *Taxi Driver* and *Broadcast News* fame, was named Albert Einstein at birth.

TRUE.

⋙⋙⋙⋙⋙⋙ **Did you know?** ⋘⋘⋘⋘⋘⋘

Paul Schrader wrote the script for *Taxi Driver* in five days and kept a loaded gun on his desk for "inspiration and motivation."

TRUE OR FALSE? Woody Allen's name at birth was Allen Kongsberg.

TRUE.

TRUE OR FALSE? Warren Beatty is older than Woody Allen.

FALSE.

   Allen is older by one year.

TRUE OR FALSE? U2's singer Bono is older than pop star Madonna.

FALSE.

   Madonna is two years older.

TRUE OR FALSE? George Clooney is older than Nicolas Cage.

TRUE.

   By two years.

TRUE OR FALSE? Courtney Cox is older than Matt Damon.

TRUE.

   By six years.

TRUE OR FALSE? Dakota Fanning is older than Justin Bieber.

FALSE.

   They are the same age.

TRUE OR FALSE? Scarlett Johansson is older than Zooey Deschanel.

FALSE.

   Deschanel is older by five years.

TRUE OR FALSE? Jay Leno is older than David Letterman.

FALSE.

   Letterman is older by four years.

TRUE OR FALSE? Al Pacino is older than singer Ted Nugent.

TRUE

> By eight years. Which only goes to show you, Al Pacino knows how to age well. The same cannot be said for Ted *Freakin'* Nugent.

TRUE OR FALSE? Demi Moore is older than Michelle Pfeiffer.

FALSE.

> Pfeiffer is older by four years.

TRUE OR FALSE? Sean Penn is older than Brad Pitt.

TRUE.

> By three years.

Q What actor and comedian was born Cornelius Crane Chase?

A Chevy Chase.

Q What actor was born Issur Danielovitch Demsky? (Hint: He's got a killer dimple.)

A Kirk Douglas.

Q What famous author was born Howard Allen O'Brien?

A Anne Rice. (Yes, you read that correctly.)

Q What actor was born Ramon Antonio Gerard Estevez?

A Martin Sheen.

Q Two of Martin Sheen's children are well-known actors. What are their names?

A Charlie Sheen and Emilio Estevez.

Q How old was Charlie Sheen when he was arrested for marijuana possession on his mother's birthday?

A Sixteen.

Q What did Charlie Sheen's parents do immediately after bailing him out of jail that day?

A Took him to church.

Q What actress was forced to wear an alcohol-monitoring device on her ankle and to attend daily alcohol-education classes in 2010?

A Lindsay Lohan.

Q What happened to Lindsay Lohan's ankle monitor when she subsequently attended an MTV Movie Awards party?

A The alarm went off.

Q What was actor David Hasselhoff wearing when he snuck out of rehab in 2002?

A Sweatpants and a tank top.

Q Where did David Hasselhoff go?

A He checked into a hotel.

Q What did David Hasselhoff do in his hotel room?

A He drank tequila from the minibar.

➡ **WHICH OF THE FOLLOWING CELEBRITIES WERE MARRIED TO EACH OTHER?**

1	Tom Cruise	A	Whitney Houston
2	Brad Pitt	B	Scarlett Johansson
3	Zac Efron	C	Jennifer Aniston
4	Ryan Reynolds	D	Angelina Jolie
5	Tiger Woods	E	Vanessa Hudgens
6	Dennis Quaid	F	Elin Nordegren
7	Sean Penn	G	Katie Holmes
8	Billy Bob Thornton	H	Meg Ryan
9	Ryan Phillippe	I	Madonna
10	Bobby Brown	J	Reese Witherspoon

ANSWERS

1G, 2C, 3E, 4B, 5F, 6H, 7I, 8D, 9J, 10A

Q How many times was Elizabeth Taylor married?

A Eight times, including twice to actor Richard Burton. Other celebrities married eight times include Mickey Rooney, Larry King, and Lana Turner.

Q Who is the most-married celebrity of all time?

A Actress Zsa Zsa Gabor, clocking in with marriages to nine different men.

Elizabeth Taylor met her seventh husband, Larry Fortensky, in rehab.

Q Who is the actress Kate Hudson's famous Oscar-winning mother?

A Goldie Hawn.

Q What's the relationship between actors Jake Gyllenhaal and Peter Sarsgaard?

A They are brothers-in-law. Sarsgaard married Jake's equally renowned sister Maggie in 2009.

Q How are Sofia Coppola and actor Nicolas Cage related?

A Cousins.

Q What's the relationship among Drew Barrymore, Steven Spielberg, and Sophia Loren?

A Speilberg and Loren are Drew Barrymore's godparents.

Q How are Shirley MacLaine and Warren Beatty related?

A Brother and sister.

Q What's the last name of these famous siblings and actors: Daniel, William, Alec, Stephen?

A Baldwin.

Q Who is the famous father of actress Zosia Mamet, who plays Shoshanna Shapiro on the HBO series *Girls*?

A Writer and director David Mamet.

Six Things You Didn't Know
≫≫≫≫≫≫≫≫≫≫≫ **About Nicolas Cage** ≪≪≪≪≪≪≪≪≪≪≪

1 Nicolas Cage's first wife was actress Patricia Arquette.

2 His second wife was Elvis's daughter, Lisa Marie.

3 His third wife, Alice Kim, is the mother of their child, Kal-El, named after the Superman character.

4 Cage's other son was the lead singer in a metal band called Eyes of Noctum.

5 At one time, Nicolas Cage had a pet octopus and two king Cobra snakes.

6 Nicolas Case prepurchased his tomb—a large pyramid—in New Orleans's famous St. Louis Cemetery #1 back in 2010.

And no, we're not making any of this up. Nicolas Cage is a weird dude.

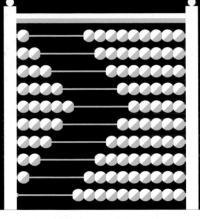

NUMBERS

. CHAPTER 15 .

Numbers

Q How many feet are in a fathom?

A Six.

Q How long is a league?

A Approximately 18,228 feet, or three miles. A league was
originally measured by how far an average person could
walk in an hour. In nautical terms, it's used to measure the
rough distance an average person could see over the horizon,
standing at sea level.

Q How long is a furlong?

A One-eighth of a mile, or 660 feet.

Q How long is a hand?

A Four inches. Oddly enough, hands are used to measure the
height of horses in many English-speaking countries.

Q How long is a cubit?

A About 18 inches. It's an ancient measurement derived from the distance between the tip of a man's middle finger and his elbow. Medieval Germans used the same unit of measure but called it an *ell*.

 **Did you know?**

How long is a Kardashian? That's a good question if you're contemplating marriage. One Kardashian equals seventy-two days—or the length of time Kim Kardashian was married to Kris Humphries.

Q How big is a flock?

A The Anglo-Saxons defined a flock as two score, or forty.

Q How heavy is a firkin?

A Fifty-four pounds. The Anglo-Saxons used it to measure butter and soap.

Q How big is an acre?

A One furlong long and 1 chain (66 feet) wide. Modern acres can be any shape, but the traditional rectangular shape of an acre comes from the amount of land a team of oxen would plough before turning around.

Q How long is a fortnight?

A Two weeks, or 1.2 million seconds if you're being precise.

Q How long is a beard second?

A Physicists actually use this measurement for incredibly small distances. Facial hair grows at an average of 10 nanometers per second, the so-called "beard second." If you're wondering, a nanometer is 1 billionth of a meter.

Q How long are a jiffy and a shake?

A "I'll be back in a jiffy," strictly speaking, means you'll be back in the amount of time it takes light to travel 1 centimeter. A shake, on the other hand, is equal to ten nanoseconds.

Did you know?

The Inca measured time by how long it took to boil a potato. It's unclear what sort of watches the Inca wore.

Q How large is a Planck unit?

A One meter equals 6.187×10^{34} Planck length units, and one second equals 1.854×10^{43} Planck time units. And if you're wondering, the speed of light equals one Planck unit. And in Plank time, the shortest moment of time that can exist is 0.00000000000000000000000000000000000000000001 second. If you are utterly confused right now, it's because you do not have a PhD in physics.

Q How long is a parsec?

A Speaking of light, a parsec is the distance light travels in roughly 3.26 light years (roughly 19 trillion miles). The closest star to Earth is a mere 1.3 parsecs away.

Q How large is an erlang?

A Erlangs are used by telecommunication companies to measure the amount of voice traffic on their network. One erlang equals one hour of continuous traffic per voice line. So two people talking on their phones nonstop for thirty minutes equals one erlang.

Q How long is a barleycorn?

A Anglo-Saxons used actual barleycorns (e.g., the length of a corn from the barley plant) as a unit of measurement—approximately 1/3 of an inch. In the Middle Ages, the inch was measured in barleycorns, with 3 barleycorns per inch.

Did you know?

The barleycorn has all but disappeared as a unit of measurement—except in shoe sizing! A size 8 shoe in the United Kingdom is exactly 1 barleycorn larger than a size 7.

Americans? We measure our shoes in inches, not barleycorns.

Q How large is a peck?

A A peck is two gallons. Pecks are still used in the United States to measure things such as grains, berries, and fruits.

Q How large is a bushel?

A A bushel in the Middle Ages measured volume and was defined as four pecks, or eight gallons. Today bushels are still used to measure commercial weights, with the weight varying by type of good being sold: A bushel of wheat is sixty pounds; a bushel of cotton is thirty-two pounds.

Q How heavy is a stone?

A Fourteen pounds. In Britain and Ireland many people measure their bodyweight in stones, despite the introduction of the metric system.

Q How big is a baker's dozen?

A Thirteen. In thirteenth-century England, bakers could be jailed—or have a hand amputated—for shortchanging customers on a "legal dozen." As a safeguard, bakers would regularly include an extra bun or muffin in each dozen. Better to be safe than handless.

Q Why is ounce abbreviated as "oz."?

A An ounce is 1/16 of a pound. The ancient Italian word for ounce was *onza*, which is where we get our modern abbreviation "oz." Never mind that modern Italians call the ounce *oncia*—the ancient name stuck.

Q Why is a pound abbreviated as "lb."?

A Blame the Romans. They called the pound a *libra*, hence our abbreviation "lb."

The number twelve is everywhere. We buy in dozens. We measure one foot as 12 inches. We have clocks that strike 12.

And yet we count in 10s. Why?

Blame it on the ancient Babylonians. Their year was approximately twelve moon cycles, or the amount of time it took to grow and harvest a crop. The Babylonians created twenty-four-hour days divided by sixty-minute hours and sixty-second minutes. And they measured circles in degrees of 360 (a factor of 12). Twelves were everywhere and highly useful to the ancient Babylonians.

If you're illiterate, however, it's easier to count in tens (ten fingers). This is the foundation of our modern Base 10 counting system, used in everything from calculating the distance to Mars to counting the value of the money in your pocket. Nowadays, tens are everywhere.

Even so, remnants of the Babylonian duodecimal (Base 12) system linger in unexpected places: count 8, 9, 10, 11, 12, 13, 14. In a pure Base 10 number system, you'd expect to count "eight, nine, ten, eleventeen, twelveteen, thirteen, fourteen"—but we don't. We count all the way to 12 before reverting to compound numbers such as 13 and 14. You have the Babylonians and their passion for Base 12 to thank for this quirk of modern counting.

Q Why does water freeze at 32°F and boil at 212°F?

A Blame the German physicist Daniel Gabriel Fahrenheit. His eighteenth-century scale for measuring heat used brine (salty water) to define the low end of the scale at 0°F, while the temperature of the human body was used to (imprecisely) define the high end of the scale at 100°F. And now we are stuck with a temperature scale that doesn't make any sense.

Q What are the only countries that officially use the Fahrenheit scale?

A The Bahamas, Belize, Cayman Islands, and the United States of America. The rest of the world uses Celsius, which sensibly freezes water at 0°C and boils water at 100°C. Some countries, including Canada, allow both Fahrenheit and Celsius scales.

TRUE OR FALSE? $111,111,111 \times 111,111,111 =$
$12,345,678,987,654,321$

TRUE.

And who says math isn't awesome?

TRUE OR FALSE? $1089 \times 9 = 9801$

TRUE.

TRUE OR FALSE? If you had a pizza with a height of "a" and a radius of "z," the volume of the pizza is pi*z^2 *a.

TRUE.

Until you eat a slice.

➤ **WHICH OF THE FOLLOWING IS TRUE?**

A $1 + 2 + 34 - 5 + 67 - 8 + 9 = 100$

B $12 + 3 - 4 + 5 + 67 + 8 + 9 = 100$

C $123 - 4 - 5 - 6 - 7 + 8 - 9 = 100$

D $123 + 4 - 5 + 67 - 89 = 100$

E $123 + 45 - 67 + 8 - 9 = 100$

F $123 - 45 - 67 + 89 = 100$

G $12 - 3 - 4 + 5 - 6 + 7 + 89 = 100$

H $12 + 3 + 4 + 5 - 6 - 7 + 89 = 100$

I $1 + 23 - 4 + 5 + 6 + 78 - 9 = 100$

J $1 + 23 - 4 + 56 + 7 + 8 + 9 = 100$

K $1 + 2 + 3 - 4 + 5 + 6 + 78 + 9 = 100$

L $-1 + 2 - 3 + 4 + 5 + 6 + 78 + 9 = 100$

M   All of the above

ANSWER

M.

TRUE OR FALSE? If 10 percent of people are gay, and you have ten kids, then one of your kids is definitely gay.

FALSE.

TRUE OR FALSE? If you have three quarters, four dimes, and four pennies, you have the largest amount of money you can have in U.S. coins without being able to make change for a dollar.

_____
TRUE.

You also have $1.19 in your pocket.

TRUE OR FALSE? There are 293 ways to make change for a U.S. dollar.

_____
TRUE.

As long as you include dollar and half-dollar coins.

TRUE OR FALSE? In the 1980s, Burma (Myanmar) switched to a Base 9 currency.

_____
MOSTLY TRUE.

Before Burmese dictator Ne Win came to power, Burma's money was issued in standard Base 10 denominations (e.g., notes of 1, 5, 10, 25, 50, and 100 kyat). In 1985, the 25-, 50-, and 100-kyat notes were declared obsolete without warning—rendering the majority of Burma's currency worthless—and replaced with an awkward 75-kyat note. Then in 1987, notes of equally awkward 45 and 90 kyats were introduced, both incorporating Ne Win's "lucky" number 9.

 **Did you know?**

After nearly bankrupting Burma with an impractical Base 9 currency, dictator Ne Win later resigned on 8-8-88, a propitious day to resign if there ever was one.

TRUE OR FALSE? The name of the search engine Google comes from the word "googol," which is the number 1 followed by one hundred zeroes.

TRUE.

The search engine was originally called "BackRub" because it looked for back links (get it?) to measure the popularity of a web page. Sensing a marketing disaster in the making, the company rechristened itself Google as a playful misspelling of "googol."

TRUE OR FALSE? A googolplex is the number 1 followed by a googol zeroes.

TRUE.

Interesting fact: A googolplex is so large it cannot be written because there's literally not enough room in the universe to fit all of those zeroes.

TRUE OR FALSE? The number 0 started life not as a number, but as a placeholder to tell the difference between 10 and 100.

TRUE.

The Babylonians used a form of 0 this way. Zero didn't become a proper number until mathematicians in India started using it in equations in the fourth and fifth centuries. In the New World, the concept of 0 was independently "discovered" a few centuries earlier by the Olmecs and possibly later by the Mayans.

TRUE OR FALSE? Numbers can be irrational, perfect, diligent, complex, composite, transcendental, imaginary, and surreal.

FALSE.

Numbers are never diligent, though they can be irrational, perfect, complex, composite, transcendental, imaginary, and surreal.

Name that Number

You've heard of millions, billions, and trillions. Now put the following larger numbers in correct ascending order:

A Vigintillion

B Quadrillion

C Septendecillion

D Septillion

E Novemdecillion

F Undecillion

G Centillion

H Nonillion

I Tredecillion

J Decillion

K Sexdecillion

L Duodecillion

M Sextillion

N Quintillion

O Quattuordecillion

P Octillion

Q Quindecillion

R Octodecillion

TRUE OR FALSE? 2 is the only even prime number.

TRUE.

TRUE OR FALSE? Prime numbers have no pattern when it comes to predicting which numbers are prime or how far apart successive prime numbers will be.

TRUE.

Prime numbers are only divisible by 1 and themselves, and there's no known pattern for when or how they will show up. Randomness is part of their beautiful mystery.

TRUE OR FALSE? 23 is the only prime number that comprises two consecutive prime numbers.

TRUE.

TRUE OR FALSE? There are an infinite number of prime numbers.

TRUE.

"Apeirophobia" is the fear of infinity.

TRUE OR FALSE? The maximum number of ways to rearrange four books on a shelf is twenty-four.

TRUE.

TRUE OR FALSE? The maximum number of ways to rearrange ten books on a shelf is 3.62 million.

TRUE.

Welcome to the power of factorials.

TRUE OR FALSE? The number 1 appears as the first digit in real-world numbers more than 30 percent of the time.

TRUE.

The number 2 is first 17.6 percent of the time, the number 3 is first 12.5 percent of the time, all the way down to the number 9—which is the first digit a mere 4.6 percent of the time. This quirk of number distribution is used to detect fraud in elections, faked scientific and economic data, false tax returns, and more.

TRUE OR FALSE? If you live in a large city and there is a 50 percent chance of rain in the forecast, it's possible there is a 0 percent chance of rain where you live.

TRUE.

Forecasts estimate the probability that 1/100th of an inch of rain will fall anywhere in the forecast area. So if there's a 100 percent chance of rain in one part of your city and a 0 percent chance of rain where you live, the probability of precipitation will be forecast as 50 percent.

TRUE OR FALSE? On average, most people have fewer friends than their friends do.

Ｔｒｕｅ.

You might think that friendship is bilateral—that you're friends with Person X and Person X is friends with you. But mathematically it's not true. The reason is simple: You are more likely to be friends with people who have more friends than with people who have fewer friends. So your friends are likely to have more friends than you. Unfortunately, the same logic holds true for sexual partners. Statistically speaking your partner has slept with more people than you have. Get over it.

TRUE OR FALSE? When you fall in love, your circle of close friends decreases by two.

Ｔｒｕｅ.

On average people have five close friends. People in romantic relationships have just three close friends, plus their new paramour. Net loss: two close friends.

TRUE OR FALSE? In a room with twenty-three people, the odds of two people sharing the same birthday is more than 50 percent.

Ｔｒｕｅ.

As long as you don't include February 29 as a potential birthday. The trick is to think about this problem in terms of pairs instead of individuals. In a room of twenty-three people there are 253 potential birthday combinations (person 1 compared to person 2, then to person 3, etc., followed by person 2 compared to person 1, person 3, etc.). So in a room of twenty-three people, the odds are slightly better than 50 percent that two people share a birthday. Increase the group size to seventy people, and the odds of two people sharing a birthday jump to 99.9 percent.

Shell Games for Beginners

Here's an interesting quirk of statistics that drives some people crazy. Assume you're playing a con game in which a pea is hidden under one of three shells. You put a finger on one shell, and the con man lifts up one of the other two shells, which is empty. The con man asks if you want to switch and pick the third shell instead of the shell your finger is currently on.

Is it in your best interest to switch and pick the third shell? The answer is yes, and always yes.

To make this work you need to assume just one thing— that the con man knows where the pea is, and he is never going to expose it to you.

In that case there's a one-third chance the pea is under the shell you selected and a two-thirds chance it's hidden under one of the other two shells. When the con man reveals one of the other two shells, the odds switch to 0 for the revealed shell and two-thirds for the other hidden shell. So you should switch! Doing so improves your odds from one-third to two-thirds. It's crazy but true.

TRUE OR FALSE? The odds of getting ten heads in a row when flipping a coin is 5 percent.

FALSE.

It's actually much smaller. Most people solve the problem by saying the odds of flipping heads each time is 50 percent, multiply that by ten flips for a 5 percent probability. In reality, this is an exponential problem: The true odds are 0.5^{10}, or about 0.1 percent.

TRUE OR FALSE? Days were only twenty-three hours long when dinosaurs roamed Earth.

TRUE.

The length of days is slowing down due to the moon's gravitational tug on Earth. Each year, Earth transfers some of its rotational momentum to the moon, which means days on Earth gain about two milliseconds per century. The upside? Weekends in the future will last longer!

TRUE OR FALSE? The world's most accurate clock will not lose even one second in a million years.

FALSE.

The National Institute of Standards and Technology in Colorado has two clocks that keep incredibly precise time—accurate to one second per *billion* years. One clock measures the vibrations of a single atom of mercury, the other is an atomic clock that "uses an aluminum atom to apply the logic of computers to the peculiarities of the quantum world." We're not sure what the latter means, but it certainly sounds accurate.

TRUE OR FALSE? The idea of standardized time didn't exist until the nineteenth century.

TRUE.

Up through the 1800s, time was a local phenomenon. Each city or village lived in its own time zone with clocks set to the local solar noon.

About the Author

SCOTT McNEELY is the author of *Ultimate Book of Sports*, *Ultimate Book of Jokes*, *Ultimate Book of Card Games*, and many other titles. He has written for numerous magazines, websites, and travel guidebooks. He lives in Portland, Oregon.